Strategic Management

Strategic Management

Core Concepts from the Internet

Brian C. Satterlee

Writers Club Press

San Jose New York Lincoln Shanghai

Strategic Management
Core Concepts from the Internet

Writers Club Press
an imprint of iUniverse.com, Inc.

For information address:
iUniverse.com, Inc.
5220 S 16th, Ste. 200
Lincoln, NE 68512
www.iuniverse.com

ISBN: 0-595-18478-2

Printed in the United States of America

This book is dedicated to the two members of my family who served as outstanding role models, both in their professional accomplishments and in their personal lives: Howard M. Gregory, my father-in-law, and William C. Satterlee III, my brother.

Contents

Foreword

As many business organizations enter the new millennium they are faced with a very complex future. Companies are now facing completely new organizational issues along with complex strategic requirements almost on a daily basis. Such issues as the changing work force as well as the actual changing management society have now become relevant strategic issues. Perhaps, the most important issue today, is how an organization will best approach increasing global competition. Also, the impact of corporate restructuring, mergers, and acquisitions, and rapid technological changes through the Internet have made it increasingly necessary for companies to quickly address the impacts and the challenges for creating new markets around the world. New strategic alliances and the emergence of new industries have now made proper planning an essential ingredient for organizational success.

The original lack of competition in years past put many companies into a sense of security and even quality during that era was a questionable condition when there was little competition. A philosophy existed to charge problems off to the customer since there was no other source for the product. As labor costs increased many organizations took the short-term approach by moving operations to where cheap labor was available. This, of course was strategy planning, however, it now appears it was a short term one. Also, during these years government and environmental controls became the planning issues, however, again appearing to be a short term planning processes meeting the demand but not actually taking any proactive approach to the issues. Over the years higher energy costs, high costs of capital, shorter product and life cycles, and increased complexity of products have all created the demand for redefinition of the economic and competitive landscape. No longer can an organization approach the future in a crisis decision manner. The challenges as well as the threats centering around some of these issues have continuously threaten to erode any long term competitive advantages of those organizations that are either slow to react or are unable to organize an effective response process.

When questioned, many representatives of present successful corporations have indicated that if an organization is expected to prosper and survive for the future, the need to build and sustain a competitive advantage must be at the top of the list. To formulate strategies using traditional ways is now said to be invalid procedures as the window of marketability for any company is getting smaller and smaller. The demand for higher levels of products/services at faster and lower costs will directly impact new competitive strategies. Thus, many of the old trade-offs associated with traditionally derived; generic competitive strategies may actually harm the future of many organizations. What happens in any location of the world now immediately affects another location of the world; therefore, planning is now rapidly becoming a redefined procedure.

Perhaps, new technologies and new distribution systems will assist in companies becoming more responsive to changing demands, however, the use of this technology in strategic planning will be impetus in building and sustaining competitive advantages. Change in how strategic planning is utilized within organizations is of the highest priority. Strategic planning is the key to both short, medium, and long term operations in the ever changing corporate world.

Dr. Lloyd Thompson
Professor of Management
February 2001

Acknowledgements

My graduate-level students contributed significantly to this project through their course participation and their reports on organizations in which they worked and conducted research. Special acknowledgement is given to Tori Callands, Catherine Campbell, James Crist, Michelle Curlee, Scotty Curlee, Miguel Guridy, Nancy Herr, Scott Justice, Richard Ruggieri, Penny Shelton, and Kristen Stanley.

Introduction

What is a Core Concept?

Many textbooks have been published in the academic field of study known *as Strategic Management*. Some are written to meet the guidelines set forth by specialized accrediting agencies; others, to impart the results of research or scholarly activities. Whatever the reason for publication, all textbooks in this field of study cover its core concepts. A core concept in a given academic discipline is one that is central to the field. All scholars may not agree that it is "correct," yet it heavily influences their thinking (through acceptance, modification, or rejection) and is likely to stand the test of time.

Tradition and the Internet

While these core concepts have stood the test of time, the application of these concepts to the professional situations of the student is in a constant state of change. How do business schools attempt to accommodate this constant state of change? Current instructional practice in most business schools is to present the core concept via an established textbook and require students to demonstrate competency in the concept by conducting a case analysis or some other experiential activity. The case study assignment requires the student to assess the situation as presented in the case, consider this assessment in light of the core concept(s) studied, and develop solutions for the case that are based on the core concept(s). In the end, students learn to apply traditional textbook-based concepts to traditional problems. Yet, as has been reported in the media, "the Internet has changed everything."

Has the Internet changed the relevancy of Strategic Management core concepts? The assumption of this book is that the relevancy of the time-tested core concepts has not changed. What the Internet has changed is access to these core concepts. It is now possible for anyone to learn the core concepts of Strategic Management, or any other field of study, via the Internet. This real-time access to information can be used to revolutionize the application of core concepts to the professional lives of those who learn them.

Limitation and Solution for Structuring Knowledge

While the Internet has revolutionized access to these core concepts, it provides no method or process for structuring this information. Thus, the information remains as is—facts and figures. When meaning and structure are added to information, knowledge is produced. Whereas the traditional textbook adds value to the learner by providing a structure to the knowledge, no such provision exists for the Internet. The purpose of this book is to provide a structure for the Internet-based study of the core concepts of Strategic Management.

Unique Learning Approach Used in This Book

Research on the known Internet information outlets has shown that current business strategy information can be fragmented, out of date, and hard to find. It was decided that the best way to approach this problem was not to try to present an extended discussion of the information itself, but to direct the prospective enquirers to a source of the required information—that is, the core concept. In essence, this book provides a short, sharp "mini-directory" of where one may learn more and structure their knowledge of these core concepts. A primary advantage of the Internet is the array of information outlets available to users. In this book, each core concept is supported by links to Websites that provide the most current information available for that topic. The questions at the end of each chapter are related to these sites, and should help the reader structure their knowledge with efficiency and purpose. Opportunities to investigate the core concept in greater depth can be realized by following the links provided from the various Websites (for each chapter).

Selection of Core Concept URLs

Each core concept Website was selected strictly for its intellectual content. Information on the Internet exists on a continuum of reliability and quality. It has been said, "knowledge is power." In the virtual environment of the Internet, only some information is power—reliable information. Source evaluation, defined as the determination of information quality, requires the use of multiple indicators to ensure quality and reliability. The indicators used to evaluate the Websites referenced in this text are: credibility (an authoritative source that supplies good evidence that allows you to trust it); accuracy (a source that is correct today—not yesterday—and gives a balanced perspective of the topic); reasonableness (engages the core concept thoughtfully and reasonably, concerned with the truth); and support (provides convincing evidence for the claims made, a source one may triangulate).

Suggestions for Internet-Based Learning

The Internet, then, is in a continual state of change and revision. Keeping up with this change can be very challenging. Fortunately, the Internet allows easy access to many of the sources needed to remain on the cutting edge of Strategic Management core concepts. The following suggestions are provided to help the reader cope with Internet-based learning:

• Understand that it is the nature of Websites to constantly change. Revisions and deletions occur daily, and sometimes the actual URL changes. Be ready to accommodate for these changes.

• Sometimes one may receive an error message such as, *"There was no response. Server could be down. Try later."* The usual culprit in these instances: too many users trying to log on at the same time. When this happens, attempt to log on again. If this doesn't work, try 20 minutes later. You should be able to eventually login the site.

- If you receive a message that the Website does not exist, try entering the URL again but omit some of the last part, i.e., enter the home address only. Once in the Website, locate the desired destination via the Site Map.

What To Do In The Event A Core Concept Website Is No Longer Available

Refer to the chapter heading that corresponds to the core concept, then use that chapter heading as a descriptor (for your favorite Search Engine) to find other sources for the particular core concept. For example, suppose the URL linking you to the topic heading, *The Benefits of Strategic Management,* is no longer active. Access a Search Engine of your choice, insert the topic heading, and search for new sites related to that heading. Be sure to employ the four criteria for source evaluation when selecting replacement URLs: credibility, accuracy, reasonableness, and support.

How To Use This Book

This book can be used by anyone interested in using the Internet to gain or improve or structure their knowledge of Strategic Management: the business practitioner, the business student, and the business school professor. Each chapter covers a specific Strategic Management core concept, which in turn, is subdivided into three topical areas. A brief discussion of each core concept and topical area is provided, along with URL's that link the reader to further investigation via the Internet. Questions for review and knowledge testing are included at the end of each chapter.

CHAPTER 1

The Challenge of Strategic Management

Strategic Management focuses on the activities of the general manager who is responsible for determining the shape and character of the total enterprise or one of its businesses, divisions, or profit centers. Those with formal strategy responsibilities are concerned with setting direction for the enterprise, determining the basis on which the organization will compete, evaluating opportunities for growth, and initiating actions that will enhance competitive performance. These activities are undertaken within an environment that is constantly changing because of technological advances, increased global competition, shifts in consumer demand, changing legal and regulatory pressures imposed by government, and actions undertaken by competitors. Within this context, the primary goal of the general manager is to effectively adapt the organization to its competitive environment.

Strategic Competitiveness and Competitive Advantages

http://www.mcmahan-group.com/news/planning.html
http://www.mcb.co.uk/courseware/mba/sm-010.htm
http://www.euro.net/innovation/Management_Base/Man_Guide_Rel_1.0B1
/C.html

The ability of a general manager to effectively adapt an organization to its competitive environment allows the organization to become more strategically competitive. The concept of strategic competitiveness implies that an organization should develop what could be termed as a strategic mindset. The creation of this strategic mentality ought to be viewed as the most important task taken by senior management. Strategic competitiveness, however, implies that the company will have to seek ways to enhance resource productivity in an effort to achieve competitive advantage.

Competitive Advantage is the ability to sell a product or service at a lower cost than your competitors and/or the ability to differentiate your product or service and charge a higher price. Competitive scope (the breadth of activities) is often used to find competitive advantage. Broad scope can allow you to exploit interrelationships between the value chains in different market segments. An example is sharing a sales force to sell two product ranges. The value chain is the process of adding value to a good or service sold by a company.

Global and Technological Change in the Evolving Competitive Landscape

http://www.iprod.auc.dk/forsk/technolo.htm
http://www.journal.au.edu/ijcim/jan99/ijcim_ar3.html

One way organizations achieve competitive advantage is through global and technological change. Introducing new technology in most enterprises requires paralleled organizational and technological development. Due to the need of this paralleled development, a situational approach should be adopted that concentrates on the following topics:

1. Strategic planning of technological development, including development of a concept as a means for integrating technological, organizational, managerial and economic aspects,
2. Planning and management of technology imposed changes, e.g. defining appropriate focal areas and milestones,
3. Management systems and their development, including the role of management systems for stimulating individual and collective learning processes,
4. Future organizational structures and forms, including the multidimensional organizational structure and organizational learning processes.

The Benefits of Strategic Management

http://www.ebs.hw.ac.uk/TEFRC/mba/sp/module1.html

Some Organizational Behavior experts maintain that it is not so much the existence of a plan which benefits the company, but the process by which a plan is developed; this process leads to relationships among employees, and approaches to the job, which would otherwise be lacking.

Company-wide knowledge of the approach to strategic management, and the process by which it is arrived at, can have a positive impact on resource allocation within the company by helping to minimize unnecessary conflict and to provide an overall sense of direction. It is difficult for managers to feel part of a team working towards a common goal when that goal is not clear to them and they do not see how their individual actions contribute to achieving it.

QUESTIONS

Strategic Competitiveness and Competitive Advantages
http://www.mcmahan-group.com/news/planning.html
http://www.mcb.co.uk/courseware/mba/sm-010.htm
http://www.euro.net/innovation/Management_Base/Man_Guide_Rel_1.0B1 /C.html
1. What are the "strategic choices" that management can make through the strategic planning process?

Global and technological change in the evolving competitive landscape
http://www.iprod.auc.dk/forsk/technolo.htm
http://www.journal.au.edu/ijcim/jan99/ijcim_ar3.html
2. According to Basant (1993), what are the three main methods for technology acquisition?

The Benefits of Strategic Management
http://www.ebs.hw.ac.uk/TEFRC/mba/sp/module1.html
3. What is the five-point plan for achieving success through strategic planning?

CHAPTER 2

Initial Political Dimensions of Strategic Management

One of the most important goals of strategic management is to help owners and managers create a clear vision for the growth of the company. Without that, it is as difficult to build a successful company as it is to build a building when you can't decide on the dimensions or number of rooms. When developing a strategic plan, consideration must be given to the various political dimensions and their influence on the planning process to achieve success. This consideration helps to assure decision-makers that their strategic intent is in accordance with the direction of the company.

Strategic Intent/Mission/Vision

http://www.npr.gov/library/papers/benchmrk/customer.html

The ability of decision-makers to assure that their strategic intent is in accordance with the direction of the company is a true sign of successful leadership. Leadership is the capacity to translate vision into reality. For organizations to translate vision into reality, top leaders must clearly convey the organization's mission, strategic direction, and vision to employees and external customers. A clear, concise statement that communicates what the organization is and is not increases the likelihood for buy-in from both employees and external customers.

Stakeholders and their Influence

http://www.walkerinfo.com/resources/publications/whitepapers/Gss1a.pdf

Buy-in from both employees and external customers is very important toe the overall success or fulfilling an organization's strategic intent. Today's business world demands that corporations be in tune with many factors to stay ahead of the game. Companies must have loyal customers who purchase again because they are satisfied and perceive value; they need to have a rewarding reputation with shareholders, financial analysts, suppliers, media and other constituents; and they must have committed employees that are willing to continue to learn and will provide outstanding service and productivity.

These groups of individuals who have a stake in or effect on a business are called stakeholders. Managing these relationships has been the topic of many recent articles, seminars and books. Corporations are adding stakeholder measurements of loyalty and commitment as leading indicators of performance alongside historical results indicators such as profit, revenue growth, and productivity.

The Work of Strategists
http://www.planware.org/strategy.htm#1

In order for strategic management to be successful, guidance must be given to insure that methods of achieving strategic intent are implemented. These methods include things such as review or preparation of a strategic plan. Without this guidance a company will loose sight of where it is trying to go. Senior business managers are often so preoccupied with immediate issues that they lose sight of their ultimate objectives. That's why a business review or preparation of a strategic plan is a virtual necessity. It is generally the role of a strategist to assist with the review and preparation of a strategic plan. Having a strategist may not be a recipe for success, but without one a business is much more likely to fail.

QUESTIONS

Strategic Intent/Mission/Vision
http://www.npr.gov/library/papers/benchmrk/customer.html
1. Define strategic direction.

Stakeholders and their Influence
http://www.walkerinfo.com/resources/publications/whitepapers/Gss1a.pdf
2. What is a stakeholder?

The Work of Strategists
http://www.planware.org/strategy.htm#1
3. A good strategy seeks to achieve what four objectives?

CHAPTER 3

The External Environment

A key premise of strategic management is that plans must be made on the basis of what has happened, is happening, and will happen in the world outside the organization with a focus on the threats and opportunities these external changes present to the organization. The external environment includes social, technological, economic, environmental, and political trends and developments.

There are two major reasons for beginning with an external analysis. First, this analysis will have implications for organizational change and development. Second, by having leaders from all functional areas of the organization involved in the analysis, it should be easier to obtain their cooperation in making adjustments in response to the external analysis.

Assessing Opportunities and Threats

http://www.cpaai.com/timely_tips_archive/june_14_1999.html
http://www-mmd.eng.cam.ac.uk/people/ahr/dstools/paradigm/swot.htm
http://www.psychwww.com/mtsite/swot.html

Opportunities and threats are both part of the external environment. Opportunities and threats are *external* factors over which the company has little control. Identifying these factors can provide valuable input to balance against strengths and weaknesses in setting strategy. You'll find most opportunities and threats in the following areas:

1. Market segments
2. Regulatory environment
3. Unmet needs
4. Competitors' positions
5. Market trends
6. Economic outlook
7. Technology
8. Customer consolidations

Scanning, Monitoring, and Forecasting

http://horizon.unc.edu/projects/seminars/futuresresearch/strategic.asp#planning
http://horizon.unc.edu/projects/seminars/futuresresearch/stages.asp
http://ophir.frcc.cccoes.edu/~IR/envrscan/scanningenvironment/03_whatis.html

To assist with the analysis of the external environment, scanning, monitoring and forecasting can be used. Environmental scanning begins with scanning the external environment for emerging issues that pose threats or opportunities to the organization. As part of this step, trends are specified that describe the issues and can be used to measure changes in their nature or significance. This stage produces a rank ordering of the issues and trends according to their importance to current or planned operations. The next stage, forecasting, focuses on developing an understanding of the expected future for the most important issues and trends. In this stage, any of the modern forecasting techniques may be used. Once the forecasts are made, each issue and trend is then monitored to track its continued relevance and to detect any major departures from the forecasts made in the preceding stage. Monitoring, in effect, identifies areas for additional and continued scanning.

Key Environmental Segments: Demographic, Economic, Legal, Political, Socio-Cultural, and Technological

http://www.buseco.monash.edu.au/Subjects/MKT/MTPonline/macro.html
http://www.buseco.monash.edu.au/Subjects/MKT/MTPonline/environment.html
http://www.accd.edu/sac/mgt/1301.090/chapter2.htm

When analyzing the external environment, one should pay particular attention to the macro environment. The macro environment relates to the larger forces that have an impact on society as a whole and not just on one or a few organizations. The macro environment includes those conditions in the external environment that can substantially influence the operations of an organization. Components of the macro environment include: demographic, economic, legal, political, socio-cultural and technological environments.

QUESTIONS

Assessing Opportunities and Threats
http://www.cpaai.com/timely_tips_archive/june_14_1999.html
http://www-mmd.eng.cam.ac.uk/people/ahr/dstools/paradigm/swot.htm
http://www.psychwww.com/mtsite/swot.html
1. List three questions to consider when assessing threats of an organization.

Scanning, Monitoring, Forecasting
http://horizon.unc.edu/projects/seminars/futuresresearch/strategic.asp#planning
http://horizon.unc.edu/projects/seminars/futuresresearch/stages.asp
http://ophir.frcc.cccoes.edu/~IR/envrscan/scanningenvironment/03_whatis.html
2. List the four procedural rules of the Delphi method of forecasting intended to overcome or minimize obstacles to effective collaborative forecasting

Key Environmental Segments: Demographics, Economic, Legal, Political, Socio-Cultural, Technological
http://www.buseco.monash.edu.au/Subjects/MKT/MTPonline/macro.html
http://www.buseco.monash.edu.au/Subjects/MKT/MTPonline/environment.html
http://www.accd.edu/sac/mgt/1301.090/chapter2.htm
3. List and briefly define three environmental conditions of the general environment.

CHAPTER 4

Industry Environmental Analysis

The organization is seldom alone in delivering its product and services to its customers. Quite the contrary, it has to often compete with several other companies. This competition is often internationalized and global. The Industry Environmental Analysis includes a thorough analysis of the five forces driving industry competition: Customers (Bargaining Power of Customers), Suppliers (Bargaining Power of Suppliers), Potential Entrants (Threat of Entry), Substitute Products (Pressure from Substitute Products or Services) and Industry Competitors (Intensity of Rivalry Among Existing Competitors). The Industry Environmental Analysis also includes an analysis of the effects on the industry of taxes and laws issued by Governments, technological development and the global as well as the local economy.

Five-Forces Model of Industry Attractiveness

http://www.collegetermpapers.com/TermPapers/Miscellaneous/five_forces.shtml
http://live.looksmart.com/cgi-
bin/framer?http://www.siue.edu/~rschult/PorterCA.htm
http://www.construct-it.salford.ac.uk/~martin/stplfirm.html
http://sol.brunel.ac.uk/~jarvis/bola/businesses/porter.html

The five-forces model is the framework in environmental analysis for analyzing determinants of industry profitability. It is used to identify the threats and opportunities confronting a company that is thinking of entering into a particular industry. The model focuses on five particular forces that Porter says shape the competition that is in each particular industry. Rivalry among established firms is the central focus that is surrounded by the threat of potential entrants and substitute technologies, as well as bargaining power of buyers and suppliers.

Strategic Group Analysis

http://www.esocrates.com/graphics/module/done/strategic%20managment/sgia
.html

To develop competitive business strategies, managers must identify important rivals and competitive threats. Strategic group analysis is useful for identifying opportunities and threats within the industry. Although all firms in an industry face the same structural forces, this does not imply that all firms will follow the same competitive strategies. In fact, each firm interprets the industry structure in light of its own objectives and resources. Each company develops its own unique competitive strategies. Thus, it is common to see many different strategic responses even within the same industry. Strategic groups in an industry are clusters of firms that follow similar strategies and compete with other clusters.

Competitor Analysis

http://ds.dial.pipex.com/town/square/ae034/competitor-analysis.shtml
http://www.lycos.com/business/cch/guidebook.html?lpv=1&docNumber=P03_2010
http://www.lycos.com/business/cch/guidebook.html?lpv=1&docNumber=P03_2011
http://www.lycos.com/business/cch/guidebook.html?lpv=1&docNumber=P03_2016
http://www.lycos.com/business/cch/guidebook.html?lpv=1&docNumber=P03_2018
http://www.lycos.com/business/cch/guidebook.html?lpv=1&docNumber=P03_2020
http://expo.entrepreneurmag.com/seminars/seminars-bizplan5.html

While strategic group analysis focuses on the rivalry amongst competitors, competitive analysis is used to determine the strengths and weaknesses of the competitors within your market, strategies that will provide you with a distinct advantage, the barriers that can be developed in order to prevent competition from entering your market, and any weaknesses that can be exploited within the product development cycle. The first step in a competitor analysis is to identify the current and potential competition. There are essentially two ways you can identify competitors. The first is to look at the market from the customer's viewpoint and group all your competitors by the degree to which they contend for the buyer's dollar. The second method is to group competitors according to their various competitive strategies so you understand what motivates them.

QUESTIONS

Strategic Group Analysis
http://www.esocrates.com/graphics/module/done/strategic%20managment/sgia
.html
1. What are mobility barriers?

Competitor Analysis
http://ds.dial.pipex.com/town/square/ae034/competitor-analysis.shtml
http://www.lycos.com/business/cch/guidebook.html?lpv=1&docNumber=P03
_2010
http://www.lycos.com/business/cch/guidebook.html?lpv=1&docNumber=P03
_2011
http://www.lycos.com/business/cch/guidebook.html?lpv=1&docNumber=P03
_2016
http://www.lycos.com/business/cch/guidebook.html?lpv=1&docNumber=P03
_2018
http://www.lycos.com/business/cch/guidebook.html?lpv=1&docNumber=P03
_2020
http://expo.entrepreneurmag.com/seminars/seminars-bizplan5.html)
2. What are the four stages in monitoring competitors?

Five-Forces Model of Industry Attractiveness
http://www.collegetermpapers.com/TermPapers/Miscellaneous/five_forces.shtml
http://live.looksmart.com/cgi-
bin/framer?http://www.siue.edu/~rschult/PorterCA.htm
http://www.construct-it.salford.ac.uk/~martin/stplfirm.html
http://sol.brunel.ac.uk/~jarvis/bola/businesses/porter.html
3. List Porter's five competitive forces.

CHAPTER 5

The Internal Environment

Human, financial, physical and technological resources define the internal environment of a business. The input of the organization is its resources. These are then transformed (either through manufacture, assembly, or some other process) into the final goods or services better known as the organization's output. There are five areas that help make up the internal environment. They include resources, capabilities, core competencies, value-chain analysis, and outsourcing.

Resources / Capabilities / Core Competencies

http://www.amsreview.org/amsrev/theory/fahy10-99.html
http://www.vernaallee.com/page23.html

One major aspect of the internal environment is resources. Resources have characteristics such as value, barriers to duplication and appropriability. A sustainable competitive advantage can be achieved if the firm

16

effectively organizes these resources in its product-markets. Resources emphasize strategic choice, charging the firm's management with the important tasks of identifying, developing and arrange key resources to maximize returns. One of the principal insights is that not all resources are of equal importance or possess the potential to be a source of sustainable competitive advantage.

Resources have three distinctive sub-groups: Tangible assets, Intangible assets, and Capabilities. Tangible assets are the fixed and current assets of the organization that contain a fixed long run capacity. They include plant, equipment, land, other capital goods and stocks, debtors and bank deposits. Tangible assets have the properties of ownership and their value is relatively easy to measure. Another defining characteristic of tangible assets is they are transparent and weak at being duplicated by competitors.

Intangible assets account for the differences that are observed between the balance sheet valuation and stock market valuation of publicly quoted companies. They include intellectual property such as trademarks and patents as well as brand and company reputation, company networks and databases. Intangible assets have relatively unlimited capacity and firms can exploit their value by using them in-house, renting them (e.g., a license) or selling them (e.g., selling a brand).

Capabilities are determined by individual or group skills as well as the organizational routines and interactions through which all the firm's resources are put together. Some examples of capabilities are teamwork, organizational culture and trust between management and workers. It is hard to place a value on capabilities because they do not have clearly defined property rights. However, the uniqueness of the individual skills makes them more difficult to duplicate.

Three types of core capabilities in an organization help define the internal environment: Vision, Understanding, and Thinking in Wholes. Vision is the ability to see a future that is different than the current reality being faced. Being able to develop and communicate a vision is a requirement that will help develop a shared vision and a shared vision is necessary discipline for the people within the organization

Understanding is a key concept in communication. There needs to be complete understanding of what is being communicated in order for the organization to have the desired outcomes. Without the ability to understand, improved outcomes diminish and it is hard to face key issues challenging our organizations today.

Thinking in wholes is a way to explain how we see the dynamics that exist in our organizations. Over the years, we have been taught to be effective without understanding all the elements that exist in our organization. Organizations are more than just collections of parts. They are parts that interact in different ways.

Core competencies are unique characteristics that make it possible for a company's internal environment to generate creative products and extend market capability. Companies that can understand these competencies are becoming leaders in their industry and will form the industry through innovation and creative new market strategies. Core competencies are the key to the future as the foundation for new products and services.

A core competency approach is somewhat different from traditional planning. In traditional planning the major emphasis is on expanding the existing business. Whereas, core competencies strategy focuses on adapting and changing to meet an uncertain future. Part of the focus includes having knowledge and skills needed to meet a variety of scenarios such as shifting markets, non-traditional customers, new technologies and political uncertainties.

A company or organization is ready to implement a competency approach when: (1) People have understood that traditional planning approaches are no longer the way for future success; (2) There is a need to reorganize business strategy, purpose and vision; or (3) There is commitment to and appreciation that this realignment requires a system focus.

Many companies do not use the language of core competencies; they use the language of the learning organization or call their approach strategic planning. There are many ways of developing core competencies, such as: (1) Clearly identify uniqueness and existing strengths; (2) Work to identify and build new knowledge and skills; and (3) Create new strengths to carry them into the future.

Value-Chain Analysis

http://www.5conf.inria.fr/fich_html/papers/p51/overview.html

The value chain analysis is a powerful resource used by strategists to diagnose and strengthen competitive advantage. Value chain analysis allows the managers to separate the underlying activities a company performs in designing, producing, marketing and distributing its product or service. It is these activities from which competitive advantage comes from.

Value chain analysis provides an appropriate framework for planning Web based businesses because it deals with the value added aspect of a system and thus helps in assessing the impact of an information technology on the business. In this concept, you need to consider every company as a collection of activities fulfilled to design, produce, market, deliver, and support its product with information technology being one main support activity for the value chain. Information systems technology is particularly pervasive in the value chain, since every value activity creates and uses information and therefore can substantially affect competitive advantage firms. If a company can find a technology that is better for performing an activity than its competitors, it will result in a competitive advantage over its competition.

In essence, value chain analysis is a form of business activity analysis, which breaks down an enterprise into its parts and helps in adopting a technology, which increases the overall profit available to a company. Value chain analysis focuses on value-adding business activities and is independent of organizational structure.

Outsourcing

http://www.firmbuilder.com/primer/article2.asp

Outsourcing applies to every aspect of today's corporation and at every level. It is a central management tool for the fundamental redesign of America's businesses. Many believe that outsourcing must be embraced by corporations if they are to compete successfully in today's global economy. It is a rethinking of what an organization is and must do itself to deliver all of its promises to customers.

Outsourcing is more than purchasing, and it is more than consulting. It is a long-term results-oriented relationship for a whole business activity over which the provider has a large amount of control and managerial discretion. Outsourcing is the use of outside business relationships to perform necessary business activities and processes in lieu of internal capabilities.

Those who provide outsourcing are often referred to as outsourcing partners, suppliers, and providers. Those who are purchasing the outsourcing services are called buyers or users. Constant interaction takes place between the user and provider. This includes a great amount of communication in which both work together to explain the services that are delivered. These services are customized to the needs of the user.

Globally, the use of outside specialized companies for everything from custodial work in hospitals in Italy to the most complex parts of the bank's business processes in Australia is increasing. Recent research suggests the growth rates of outsourcing are averaging between 25%-30% annually.

Throughout the world and the U.S., organizations are redefining themselves through outsourcing. Businesses changing from vertical to virtual is profound and greatly impacts the future success and expectations placed on every executive.

QUESTIONS

Resources / Capabilities / Core Competencies
http://www.amsreview.org/amsrev/theory/fahy10-99.html
http://www.vernaallee.com/page23.html
1. Name three types of core capabilities in an organization.

Value-Chain Analysis
http://www.5conf.inria.fr/fich_html/papers/p51/overview.html
2. List the benefits of a value-chain analysis.

Outsourcing
http://www.firmbuilder.com/primer/article2.asp
3. Explain the role of outsourcing in today's corporation.

CHAPTER 6

Strategic Importance of the Customer

Strategic importance of the customer primarily deals with customer service. Customer service is a phrase that applies to a state of mind in which you and your employees are constantly thinking about improving every facet of your business which touches customers. Customer service is finding a way to make sure every customer is satisfied and continues to do business with you. To meet the needs of your customers, you must know what the customers want and expect. You must be able to provide quality service on a consistent basis. Many companies formalize customer service plans without ever consulting their customers but this is not an effective practice. You must speak to your customers to ascertain their perception of the service you provide; in reality the customer is the ultimate critic. In addition, you must periodically ask your customers how you are doing.

In a customer service plan, you must identify the organizational customers and include a method for measuring and tracking customer satisfaction and loyalty in order to identify satisfiable customer needs. Regardless of the size of your company, you need a formal customer service plan that includes not only customer service policies and procedures, but also specific explanations on how your staff should act in a variety of situations which will help identify the core competencies required to satisfy customer needs.

Identifying Organizational Customers

http://www.britannica.com/bcom/eb/article/6/0,5716,118166+7+109821,00. html

Business marketing, sometimes called business-to-business marketing or industrial marketing, involves those marketing activities and functions that are targeted toward organizational customers. This type of marketing involves selling goods (and services) to organizations (public and private) to be used directly or indirectly in their own production or service-delivery operations. One of the key points that differentiate business from consumer marketing is the magnitude of the transactions.

Organizational customers can be broken down into three groups: user customers, original-equipment manufacturers, and resellers. User customers make use of the goods they purchase in their own businesses. An automobile manufacturer, for example, might purchase a metal-stamping press to produce parts for its vehicles. Original-equipment manufacturers incorporate the purchased goods into their final products, which are then sold to final consumers (*e.g.,* the manufacturer of television receivers buys tubes and transistors). Industrial resellers are middlemen—essentially wholesalers but in some cases retailers—who distribute goods to user customers, to original-equipment manufacturers, and to other middlemen. Industrial-goods wholesalers include mill-supply houses, steel warehouses, machine-tool dealers, paper jobbers, and chemical distributors

Identifying Satisfiable Customer Needs
http://www.office.com/global/0%2C2724%2C509-17425%2CFF.html

Organizations often claim to know their customers without ever taking the time to perform a thorough analysis of their customers' satisfaction with the services or products provided. Often potential areas of customer complaints can be realized by reviewing the return rate of products you sell. If this is high, your customers may be unhappy with their purchases, and you must find out why. Is your product inferior or not user-friendly? One can assess the number of service or maintenance calls that are received and conduct an analysis of consistency among complaints. Are the complaints related to inadequate support, faulty products or parts problems? Check the status of product shortages; if a shortage exists, there are undoubtedly unhappy customers out there. These different aspects help in identifying what the customer needs to be satisfied.

It would behoove all employers to listen to their employees when it comes to customer service. Your employees are often the ones in contact with the customers on a daily basis. It is not unusual for the first person to have contact with customers to be the receptionist. And he or she is likely to have an excellent idea of the customers' likes and dislikes. Often customers will complain about the poor quality of a product, the lack of support, or the extraordinary amount of time that they spend waiting for service from your organization. The customer or client will often not voice the complaint to others in your company. Find out from your employees what the customer complaints are. Keep in mind that only 2 percent to 4 percent of disgruntled individuals register complaints.

Having a written customer service plan will allow employees to have a source to turn to whenever they have a question about how to handle a client. The following steps will help in satisfying customer needs.

1. Recognize your organization's need for a customer service plan.
2. Determine the level of service needed.

3. Establish goals for the plan for what you want to accomplish.

4. Measure the level of consumer and business-to-business satisfaction with tools like verbal feedback, formal surveys, number of referrals, etc.

5. Create benchmarks, such as a target rate of repeat customer purchases, to measure the plan's effectiveness.

6. Adjust the plan accordingly when new information is learned.

The method of communication is as important as what is communicated. Greet your customers appropriately, make them comfortable from the beginning. The initial customer contact is very important, and first impressions can often win or lose a customer. Make your customers feel special. Listen to them attentively, find out what they like or dislike. Ask if you can help your customers. Be constructive at all times, avoid being defensive, and never lose your temper. Ask customers to give you letters or verbal recommendations or referrals. Invite your customers back to your office, store or business.

Identifying Core Competencies Required to Satisfy Customer Needs

http://www.office.com/global/0%2C2724%2C509-17425%2CFF.html

In years past, the customer service plans of many companies consisted of hiring one or two people whose job it was to handle crises that arose from disgruntled customers. Today, smart business owners know that customer service should consist of more than just a couple of people "putting out fires." Rather, it should be an ongoing effort by all employees that occurs when clients are satisfied and even when they are not. The key to making this proactive approach work is achieving buy-in from all employees, from top-level managers down to receptionists. Each staff member should understand how his or her job fits into the company's overall customer service plan—only then will they realize that every interaction with customers affects the way those customers see the company as a whole. For example, if a customer calls for the first time to inquire about a new product and encounters an abrasive switchboard operator, that may be enough to form a negative opinion of your firm, and he may never call again. Likewise, your sales staff may be high-powered deal-closers, yet lose accounts because they don't pay attention to small details like sending thank-you notes to clients.

Core competencies are unique characteristics that make it possible for a company's internal environment to satisfy customer needs. The following competencies would be required to accomplish customer satisfaction.

1. Develop a service vision in what you want your company to represent.

2. Recognize and reward employees who outperform stated customer satisfaction objectives and goals, and those who make recommendations on how to handle customer complaints better, how to be more effective, or who consistently offers better policies and procedures.

3. Hold regular "customer satisfaction" meetings and ask employees what else they recommend doing to increase customer satisfaction and establish stronger loyalty from customers.

4. Focus groups are also a popular method to gather customer information.

5. Your staff must understand and buy into the organization's service vision and customer service plan. Time must be set aside for staff education and orientation.

Each time a customer interacts with your company—whether it is to place an order, make an inquiry, return a product or lodge a complaint—there is a flow path that can be charted. Charting the customer interaction path not only increases efficiency but also assigns employees responsibility for each part of the process. By devising this pattern, your employees can handle every customer interaction in the same consistent fashion. If there's a bottleneck in the system due to consistent mistakes that are made, the flow chart will show it quickly.

Large companies typically have a flow chart in place for every conceivable customer interaction so that employees know how to behave each time they come across them. As problems arise, the chart is revised to keep the flow smooth and to alert new employees how to handle the unexpected. Small firms can learn from this technique of efficient customer service.

QUESTIONS

Identifying Organizational Customers
http://www.britannica.com/bcom/eb/article/6/0,5716,118166+7+109821,00.html
1. List the three groups that organizational customers can be broken down into.

Identifying Satisfiable Customer Needs
http://www.office.com/global/0%2C2724%2C509-17425%2CFF.html
2. What are four steps that help satisfy customer needs?

Identifying Core Competencies Required to Satisfy Customer Needs
http://www.office.com/global/0%2C2724%2C509-17425%2CFF.html
3. Explain the four core competencies that are required for companies to accomplish customer satisfaction.

CHAPTER 7

Corporate Level Strategy

Corporate-level strategy is the entire managerial game plan for a diversified company. It consists of how a diversified company can establish business positions in different industries and the actions and approaches employed to improve the performance of the group of businesses the company has diversified into. Within this strategy, diversification is a major element that is created by management to develop a multi-business strategy, which includes mergers and acquisitions. Management also changes its business strategy to restructuring in order to improve future operations.

Related and Unrelated Diversification
http://www.csuchico.edu/mgmt/strategy/module7/sld025

Diversification is related when a firm has several lines of business that, although distinct, contains some kind of strategic fit. Common Approaches to Related Diversification include:

1. Entering businesses where sole force, advertising, and distribution activities can be shared.
2. Taking advantage of closely related technologies.
3. Sharing manufacturing facilities.
4. Transferring the knowledge from one business to another.
5. Transferring firm's brand name and reputation with consumers to a new product or service.
6. Acquiring new businesses to help firm's position in existing businesses.

Related diversification may be appealing as a strategy, since it enables the firm to:

1. Maintain unity in business activities and gain benefits of skills transfer or cost sharing while spreading risks over broader base.
2. Take advantage of a firm in what it does best and allows transfer of core competencies from one business to another.
3. Achieve economies of scope.
4. Develop strategic fits among related businesses, thus offering competitive advantage potential of lower costs via sharing common resources and combining related activities.
5. Allow efficient transfer of key skills or core competencies.
6. Employ the common use of some brand name.

Unrelated Diversification involves no common linkage of strategic fit among a diversified firm's lines of business. It also involves no meaningful value chain interrelationships. The dominant philosophy of unrelated diversification is that any company can be acquired on good financial terms and offers good prospects for profitability is a good business to diversity into. The appeal of Unrelated Diversification includes:

1. Business risk scatter over different industries.
2. Capital resources invested in those industries offering best profit prospects.
3. Stability of profits.

If management is exceptionally well at finding bargain-priced firms with big profit potential then shareholder wealth can be enhanced.

Drawbacks of Unrelated Diversification include:

1. More diverse the businesses, the harder it is to oversee each subsidiary and spot problems.
2. Promises greater soles-profit stability over business cycles, but is seldom realized.

Mergers and Acquisitions

http://www.britannica.com/bcom/eb/article/2/0,5716,108722+19+106110,00 .html

Companies often grow by combining with other companies. In mergers and acquisitions, one company may purchase all or part of another; two companies may merge by exchanging shares; or a wholly new company may be formed through consolidation of the old companies. From the financial manager's viewpoint, this kind of expansion is like any other investment decision: the acquisition should be made if it increases the acquiring firm's net present value as reflected in the price of its stock.

The most important term that must be negotiated in a combination is the price the acquiring firm will pay for the assets it takes over. Present earnings, expected future earnings, and the effects of the merger on the rate of earnings growth of the surviving firm are perhaps the most important determinants of the price that will be paid. Current market prices are the second most important determinant of prices in mergers: depending on whether or not asset values are indicative of the earning power of the acquired firm, book values may exert an important influence on the terms of the merger.

A merger may be treated as either a purchase or a pooling of interests. In a purchase, a larger firm generally takes over a smaller one and assumes all management control. The amount actually paid for the smaller firm is reflected in the acquiring firm's balance sheet; if more was paid for the acquired firm than the book value of its assets, the difference is reflected in the acquiring firm's financial statements as goodwill. In a pooling of interests, the merged firms are usually about the same size; both managements carry on important functions after the merger; and common stock, rather than cash or bonds, is used in payment. The total assets of the surviving firm in a pooling are equal to the sum of the assets of the two independent companies, and no surplus remains to be written off as a charge against earnings.

The basic requirements for the success of a merger are that it fit into a soundly conceived long-range plan and that the resulting firm has performance characteristics superior to those attainable by the previous companies independently. In the heady environment of a rising stock market, mergers have often been motivated by superficial financial aims. Companies with stock selling at a high price relative to earnings have found it advantageous to merge with companies having a lower price-earnings ratio; this enables them to increase their earnings per share, thus appealing to investors who purchase stock on the basis of earnings.

In mergers, one firm disappears. An alternative is for one firm to buy all or a majority of the voting stock of another and to run it as an operating subsidiary. The acquiring firm is then called a holding company. There are several advantages in the holding company: it can control the acquired firm with a smaller investment than would be required in a merger; each firm remains a separate legal entity, and the obligations of one are separate from those of the other; and stockholder approval is not necessary, as it is in the case of a merger. There are also disadvantages to holding companies, including the possibility of multiple taxation and the danger that the high rate of leverage will amplify the earnings fluctuations of the operating companies.

Corporate Restructuring

http://www.nysscpa.org/cpajournal/old/17285144.htm

In a restructuring, the corporation changes its business strategy or structure to improve future operations. Restructuring often include an overabundance of items including the costs of employee severance and termination, costs to eliminate or curtail product lines, costs to consolidate or relocate operations, costs for new systems development or acquisition, losses relating to asset impairments, and losses on disposal of assets.

Corporations have frequently reported restructuring charges in the period in which the decision to restructure was made. Such practice was becoming increasingly widespread according to the EITF. The SEC found that restructuring charges at times included expenditures that would benefit future continuing operations, such as expenditures for equipment, costs associated with relocating and retraining employees, advertising and legal costs, charges for consulting services, and increased warranty liabilities on sales not yet made.

In accounting for a restructuring, the primary issues are the costs to be classified as restructuring and the timing of the recognition of these costs. While current GAAP provides some guidance in the recognition of restructuring charges, existing literature fails to provide a pathway for uniform practice. As stated in EITF 94-3, these issues provided the impetus for current discussions:

Although the accounting for some costs that have been included in restructuring charges, such as employee severance and termination costs, is addressed in existing accounting pronouncements, it is not always clear when those costs should be recognized if they arise in connection with a restructuring. The existing accounting pronouncements also do not address directly the accounting for other costs that may be incurred as part of a formally adopted restructuring plan, such as costs to consolidate or relocate plant facilities. There appears to be diversity in practice in recognizing those costs.

A restructuring may be considered complete when certain specific events have taken place including, for example, when all:

1. planned employee terminations have occurred,
2. operations identified for closure in the plan of restructuring have ceased,
3. assets identified for sale have been disposed of, and
4. exit costs have been paid.

QUESTIONS

Related and Unrelated Diversification
http://www.csuchico.edu/mgmt/strategy/module7/sld025
1. Identify at least 3 advantages of related diversification.

Corporate Restructuring
http://www.nysscpa.org/cpajournal/old/17285144.htm
2. In restructuring, the corporation changes its business strategy or structure to improve future operations and often include…

Mergers and Acquisitions
http://www.britannica.com/bcom/eb/article/2/0,5716,108722+19+106110,00.html
3. Explain what a merger is and the requirements needed for its success.

CHAPTER 8

Business-Level Strategy

Business-Level Strategy deals with the actions and the approaches created by management to produce successful achievement in one specific area of business. The overall idea of this strategy is to create and strengthen the company's long-term competitive position in the business world.

Basically, business-level strategy involves whatever moves or new approaches managers require in light of market forces, economic trends and developments, buyer needs, and demographics, new legislation and regulatory requirements, and other various external factors. Three important business level strategies used by companies are cost leadership, differentiation, and focus.

Cost Leadership Strategies
http://zzyx.ucsc.edu/!boxjenk/cos/tsld008.htm

A low-cost leadership strategy is when you open up a sustainable cost advantage over competitors by using a lower-cost edge as a basis to under-price competitors and gain market share or build a greater profit by selling at the regular price. The characteristics of a low-cost provider are:

1. Cost conscious corporate culture
2. Employee participation in cost-control effects
3. Ongoing efforts to benchmark costs
4. Intensive scrutiny of budget requests
5. Progress promoting continuous cost improvement.

In order to achieve low-cost leadership, company managers should scrutinize every cost-creating activity and identify cost drivers. They must use knowledge about cost drivers in order to control costs of each activity year after year. Finding ways to reengineer how activities are performed and coordinated (get rid of unnecessary work steps) will also achieve low-cost leadership. Company managers will need to be creative in cutting some activities out of the value chain system (re-invent the industry value chain) to achieve low-cost leadership.

Strengths of low-cost leadership include:

1. Better positioned than rival competitors to compete offensively on basis of price
2. Low-cost provides some protection from bargaining leverage of powerful buyers
3. Low-cost provides some protection from bargaining leverage of powerful suppliers
4. Low-cost provider's pricing power acts as a significant barrier for potential entrants
5. Low cost puts a company in position to use low price as a defense against substitutes

A low-cost strategy works best when price competition is vigorous and when the product is standardized or readily available from many suppliers. The strategy also works best when there are a few ways to achieve differentiation that have value. Furthermore, a low cost strategy works best when most buyers use a product in the same way, when buyers incur low switching costs, and when buyers are large and have significant bargaining power.

Weaknesses of low-cost strategies:

1. Being overly aggressive in cutting prices (revenue erosion of lower price is not offset by gains in sales volume—profits go down, not up)
2. Rivals easily imitate low cost methods
3. Becoming too focused on reducing costs and ignoring:

Differentiation Strategies

http://zzyx.ucsc.edu/~boxjenk/C05/tsld018.htm

Differentiation Strategies incorporate differentiating features that cause buyers to prefer firm's product or service over the brands of rivals. The key to this strategy is finding ways to differentiating that will create value for buyers and that are not easily matched or cheaply copied by rivals. Also, not spending more to achieve differentiation than the price premium that can be charged. Successful differentiation is achieved when a product/service with unique and appealing attributes allows a firm to command a premium price, increase unit sale, and build brand loyalty.

There are several strengths of differentiation strategy. One strength is buyers develop loyalty to brands they like best which beat rival competitors in the market. Another strategy is mitigation of bargaining power of large buyers since other products are less attractive. Differentiation puts a seller in better position to withstand efforts of suppliers to raise prices and to fend off threats of substitutes not having comparable features. The buyer loyalty also acts as a barrier to potential entrants.

Differentiation strategy works best when there are many ways to differentiate a product that have value and please customers and when buyer needs and uses are diverse. It is successful when few rivals are following a similar type of differentiation approach and when technological change is fast paced and competition is focused on evolving product features.

What can cause a differentiation strategy to fail?

1. Trying to differentiate on a feature buyers do not perceive as lowering their cost or enhancing their well-being
2. Over-differentiating such that product features exceed buyer's needs
3. Charging a price premium that buyers perceive is too high
4. Failing to signal value
5. Not understanding what buyers want or prefer and differentiating on the "wrong" things

Focus Strategies
http://zzyx.ucsc.edu/~boxjenk/C05/tsld032.htm

Focus Strategies involve concentrated attention on a narrow piece of the total market. The key to success is to choose a market niche where buyers have distinctive preferences, special requirements, or unique needs. Develop unique capabilities to serve needs of target buyer segment. What makes a niche attractive for focusing?

1. Big enough to be profitable
2. Good growth potential
3. Not crucial to success of major competitors (making it unlikely they will compete hard in niche)
4. Focuser has resources to effectively serve segment
5. Focuser can defend against challengers via superior ability to serve buyers in segment and customer goodwill

Strengths of focus strategies include:

1. Rival competitors do not have matching capabilities to meet specialized needs of niche members
2. Focuser's competencies/capabilities act as a barrier to potential entrants
3. Focuser's unique ability to meet niche buyers' needs can blunt bargaining leverage of powerful buyers .

When does a focus strategy work best?

1. Costly or difficult for multi-segment rivals to serve specialized needs of target niche
2. No other rivals are concentrating on same segment
3. Firm's resources do not allow it to go after a bigger piece of market
4. Industry has many different segments, creating more focusing opportunities

Risks of a focus strategy are:

1. Competitors find effective ways to match a focuser's capabilities in serving niche
2. Niche buyers' preferences shift towards product attributes desired by majority of buyers—the niche becomes part of the overall market
3. Segment becomes so attractive it becomes crowded with rivals, causing segment profits to be splintered

QUESTIONS

Cost Leadership Strategies
http://zzyx.uscs.edu/!boxjenk/cos/tsld008.htm
1. List four strengths of low-cost leadership.

Differentiation Strategies
http://zzyx.uscs.edu/~boxjenk/co5/tsld018.htm
2. List four reasons that make a differentiation strategy fail.

Focus Strategies
http://zzyx.uscs.edu/~boxjenk/cos/tsld032.htm
3. Explain when a focus strategy works best and the risks that are involved.

CHAPTER 9

Cooperative Strategies

Cooperative Strategies are actions such as partnerships, joint ventures, alliances, collaboration, outsourcing, franchising, and consortia. The primary approach to cooperative strategies include both strategic alliances and network strategies.

Rationale for Entering into Cooperative Business Arrangements

http://mgmt.tamu.edu/mgmt.www/m-hill/formulating_cooperative_strategy.html
http://www.wisc.edu/uwcc/icic/orgs/ica/struc/Regional-Offices1/Regional-Office-for-Asia-and-Pacific1/Asia—Co-op-Dialogue—Vol—7—No—3—1991/Effective-Co-operative-System-towards-Tw1.html

Cooperative business arrangements allow firms to use both strategic alliances and network strategies to successfully pursue mutual business interests. The rationale for entering into cooperative business arrangements include sharing risk, gaining market power, and gaining access to new markets. The two concentrations of cooperative strategies are listed below.

Strategic Alliances

http://www.entrepreneurs.about.com/smallbusiness/entrepreneurs/library/week ly/aa061500a.htm
http://www.mcg-invest.dk/mcg-gb-strategic-alliances-joint-ventures.htm

Strategic alliances are partnerships between firms who combine their resources, capabilities, and core competencies in order to pursue mutual interests, such as:

1. Gain access to markets, ideas and materials
2. Gain market power (be larger and stronger)
3. Speed up development or entry into a market
4. Share risk of new products, markets

Various forms of strategic alliances include:

1. Business-Level Cooperative Strategies
2. Complementary Alliances—each partner provides complementary resources. Examples: vertical integration, horizontal integration, outsourcing
3. Competition Reduction strategies—mutual forbearance. Examples: cartel, "gentlemen's agreements," government policy. Illegal example: price fixing.

4. Competition Response strategies—partners ally to gain power in a competitive industry. Example: alliances between software, cable, phone companies.

5. Uncertainty Reduction strategies—partners ally to increase flexibility and effectiveness of response in a n uncertain environment. Example: telecommunications deregulation.

Corporate-level Cooperative Strategies may be further classified:

1. Diversifying—firms can move into new areas without a merger or acquisition. Example: Disney goes into the web portal business by agreement with InfoSeek.

2. Synergistic—firms can get synergy effects without a merger or acquisition. Example.: Microsoft shares its operating and applications software code with independent software dependent companies, and they produce products that complement MS products.

3. Franchising—the franchising firm diversifies into the new markets without assuming the financial risk. Example: any franchise retail outlet.

Risks of Cooperation include:

1. Difficulty managing the resulting venture

2. Cheating—partners may use the alliance to compete against each other, or partners may misrepresent themselves to each other

3. Trustworthiness—having it, and identifying it in others

Network Strategies
http://www.internetwk.com/trends/trends111698.htm

Network strategies are actions taken to increase the quality and quantity of business through networking. Networking is a tool that lets independent departments share information allowing the company to act as one. The following are examples of Network Strategy Methods:

1. Internet technology (e-mail/Internet search capabilities) that allow cost effective sharing of external information internally without the use of several lines

2. Installing a network for printer sharing to avoid cost associated with multiple printers

3. Intra-net technology that allow departments to effectively communicate internally within an organization

QUESTIONS

Strategic Alliances
http://mgmt.tamu.edu/mgmt.www/m-hill/formulating_cooperative_strategy.html
http://www.entrepreneurs.about.com/smallbusiness/entrepreneurs/library/weekly/aa061500a.htm
1. Define what is meant by a strategic alliance.
2. How can a competition reduction strategy be considered illegal?

Network Strategies
http://www.internetwk.com/trends/trends111698.htm
3. Define what is meant by network strategies.
4. How can network strategies help to improve business?

Strategic Alliances

(http://mgmt.tamu.edu/mgmt.www/m-hill/formulating_cooperative_strategy.html)

(http://www.entrepreneurs.about.com/smallbusiness/entrepreneurs/library/weekly/aa061500a.htm

5. Explain what the goal of strategic alliances is and what they are meant to accomplish.

CHAPTER 10

International Strategy

International Strategy is action taken to create value by transferring valuable skills and products to foreign markets where indigenous competitors lack those skills and products. Most international firms create value by transferring differentiated product offerings developed at home to new markets overseas.

Identifying International Opportunities

http://www.nike.com/
http://www.toyota.co.jp/index-n.html

Globalization is the driving force behind International business strategies. An increasingly globalized world is dramatically changing today's economic landscape. Kumar & Subramaniam in *Journal of World Business*, (Spring 1997) state that with a significantly large number of countries welcoming foreign investment and an increasing number of firms implementing global strategies, the nature of international business is undergoing dramatic transformation. Factors such as severe domestic competition, lesser lead times for innovation and the high cost of new product development have led firms to consider entering new markets as a viable growth strategy. Hence, there has been a rapid increase in the number of companies trying to enter foreign markets.

When a firm decides to expand internationally, it has to choose the foreign market it wants to operate. The market selection decision involves choosing the best country market to enter based on the strategic needs and orientation of the firm. Once the firm has decided to enter a foreign market, it has to determine the nature of its operations in the foreign market. Reasons for deciding to enter the foreign market include extending the product life cycle, securing essential resources and have access to low-cost labor (NAFTA is an example).

The nature of the firm's operations in the country market depends on its choice of mode of entry. A mode of entry is an institutional arrangement chosen by the firm to operate in the foreign market. This decision is one of the most critical strategic decisions for the firm. It affects all the future decisions and operations of the firm in that country market. Since each mode of entry entails a concomitant level of resource commitment, it is difficult to change from one entry mode to another without considerable loss of time and money.

Firms have adopted a number of different modes to enter foreign markets. They have been classified based on their risk, return characteristics and the degree of control the mode provides the entrant. The different modes of entry have been classified into exporting, contractual agreements, joint ventures, acquisitions, and Greenfield investments. Exporting involves only the physical transfer of goods from the firm to the foreign market with or without an agent in exchange for the value of the goods in monetary terms. Contractual Agreement is a binding contract between the firm and an agent to produce and distribute the goods in the foreign market in return for some form of economic rents. A Joint Venture is the pooling of assets and (or) knowledge by two or more firms who share joint ownership and control over the results of the pooling. Note that this definition includes both joint ventures and strategic alliances as defined in the traditional sense. Acquisition refers to the purchase of stock in an already existing company in an amount sufficient to exercise control. Greenfield investment is a start up investment in new facilities in the foreign market.

International business level strategies are similar to the generic business level strategy types: international low cost, international differentiation, international focus, and international integrated low cost/differentiation. However, each of the strategies is usually grounded in some home country advantage. The advantages may be factors of production, demand conditions, related and supporting industries and patterns of firm strategy, structure and rivalry.

International strategies have three primary classifications: a multi-domestic strategy focuses on competition within each country in which the firm operates. Firms employing this strategy decentralize strategic and operating decisions to the strategic business units operating in each country so each can tailor its goods and services to the local market. A global strategy assumes more standardization of products across country boundaries. Therefore, competitive strategy is centralized and controlled by the home office. A transnational strategy seeks to combine aspects of both multi-domestic and global strategies in order to emphasize both local responsiveness and global integration and coordination. Many large multi-national firms, particularly those with diverse product lines, many use a multi-domestic strategy with some products and global strategy with others.

It has been assumed in the literature that managers of firms have unlimited time and monetary resources to gather the required information to make an optimal, rational decision. But there are many instances when managers are faced with constraints that prevents them from undertaking an elaborate information search necessary for arriving at an optimal decision. Past research on the mode of entry, decision does not offer any insights into decision making under such constrained situations.

The decision on how to conduct business in a foreign country depends not only on various factors, many of which have been studied in the past literature, but also on the time and resource constraints that the manager faces when he/she makes the decision. Hence, the resource and time constraints for making the decision itself may lead a manager to sub-optimize.

Categories of decision strategies running from analytic strategies such as maximization of expected utility to non-analytic strategies such as flipping a coin or just repeating a previous response. The range differs primarily on two dimensions: (a) the amount of resources required to use each strategy and (b) the ability of each strategy to produce an "accurate" response. Some strategies may involve elaborate and costly information collection and processing while some may be based on simple heuristics. The final stage of this process is the actual decision choice as to which mode of entry to use when entering the foreign market.

The choice of a decision strategy is also contingent upon the characteristics of the decision-maker and the characteristics of the decision task. Further, the choice of a decision strategy is dependent on the manager's prior expectation of the quality of information he/she can obtain. If the manager does not expect to obtain accurate, reliable and valid information then he/she will choose a decision strategy that will require lesser information gathering and processing. Since strategy selection is a subjective process, the influence of the decision task characteristics on it is mediated by the decision-maker's perception of those characteristics. Moreover, personality variables may affect the final choice of a particular mode but not the selection of decision strategies. However, there are a number of characteristics that can differentiate among decisions only a few of the characteristics that are important for selection of a strategy to include unfamiliarity, ambiguity, complexity, and instability.

Choice of International Entry Mode

http://www.hoechst.com

Most executives contend that as they have looked across the seas, overcoming sales, marketing, and related financing challenges has been—and will continue to be—extraordinarily difficult. Companies need to study the logistics of expanding overseas before simply tabulating the potential for profit. To help, firms should ask the following three questions. The answers may determine whether doing business abroad is in the best interest of your company.

Do You Have A Legitimate International Strategy? Regardless of a company's size, the most important challenge is the same: Developing a long-term international strategic plan that has the full support of senior management. That plan can go out as far as five or six years. The plan must examine whether there's a demand for existing or new products, and if so, where; how the company will sell its products abroad, either through its own sales force or, most likely, through distributors or agents; realistic timelines for international sales growth; and how that growth will be funded. The strategic plan might consider a number of important marketing and sales issues. For instance, is product tailoring needed to meet the specific tastes and norms regarding packaging, colors, sizes, and language?

Who Will Distribute Your Product? If many companies don't understand the importance of strategic planning, product adaptation, and senior management commitment, they at least know that they must establish optional sales and distribution channels if they're going 'to succeed. Only the largest companies, those with at least $500 million in sales, consider the possibility of setting up their own sales teams and offices abroad; fewer yet can afford to set up joint or equity partnerships with major firms or governments abroad where sales and distribution channels and talent can be shared. The rest must rely on finding the right distributor or agent in individual countries or regions to handle their products. Too often, though, companies fail to research the alternatives as thoroughly as they should or ask all the necessary questions.

Can You Find the Right Partner? Those with the best distributor or agent deals understand that the arrangement must be two-way to succeed.

Some firms indeed decide to compete only in certain regions of the world, as opposed to viewing all markets in the world as potential opportunities. Competing regionally allows firms to focus their learning on specific markets, cultures location resources, etc. As stated above, firms may enter markets in several ways to include exporting, licensing, forming alliances with local partners, managing acquisitions, and establishing new, subsidiaries. Most firms, due to cost and risk, began with exporting or licensing. The most expensive and risky means of entering a new international market is through the establishment of a new wholly owned subsidiary, but this method does offer maximum control and potentially, greatest returns.

International diversification offers an opportunity for innovation, larger market size and may generate the resources necessary to sustain a large-scale research and development program.

Problems Associated with International Expansion
http://strategis.ic.gc.ca/SSG/bo01033e.html

Indeed, international markets offer greater economies of scope and learning as well as above average return potential. Risks to international strategies include political problems (unstable governments) and economic risks (currency fluctuations). Other down sides are coordination and distribution difficulties, management problems that are heightened by trade barriers, logistical costs and cultural diversity. Lastly, international markets are highly competitive and relationships/partnerships with the local providers and government is essential.

QUESTIONS

Identifying international opportunities:
http://www.nike.com/
http://www.toyota.co.jp/index-n.html
1. _____ is the driving force behind International business strategies.

Choice of international entry mode
http://www.hoechst.com
2. Greenfield investments refers to what concept?
3. Go to URL: *http://nikebiz.com/community/index.shtml* & visit their global facts page to discuss Nike's involvement in the global community.

CHAPTER 11

Corporate Governance

The subject of corporate governance is huge and varied (refer to *http://www.oecd.org/daf/governance/principles.htm*). The research in this area is rapidly increasing. The concept of corporate governance is poorly defined because it covers a large number of distinct economic areas. The different definitions reflect special interest in the field. Issues of corporate governance—junk bonds, corporate takeovers, downsizing, executive pay, the rise of pension funds—are discussed daily in the press. Therefore, what has changed and how can it lead to more effective and responsible, corporate leadership?

Corporate governance deals with the ways in which suppliers of finance to corporations assure themselves of getting a return on their investment. It is a system by which business corporations are directed and controlled. It specifies the distribution of rights and responsibilities among different participants in the corporation, such as, the board, managers, shareholders and other stakeholders, and spell out the rules and procedures for making decisions on corporate affairs. Its framework depends on the legal, regulatory, and institutional environment. By doing this, it also provides the structure through which the company objectives are set and the means of attaining those objectives and monitoring performance (refer to the following website for a Statement on Corporate Governance for the Tandy-Corporation (*http://www.tandy.com/investor/investor_corp_governance.htm*).

Corporate governance, the nuts-and-bolts of how a public company fulfills its responsibilities to investors and other stakeholders, is frequently overlooked in debates over corporate social responsibility. Despite its still relatively low profile, it's where much of the real action is going on when it comes to positively changing corporate behavior and ethical considerations of the board of directors and the separation of ownership and managerial control.

Separation of Ownership and Managerial Control
http://www.geocities.com/WallStreet/Floor/3935/j-firm.html

One of the obvious and significant successes of corporate governance advocates is in the area of director independence. It was recognized that an independent mechanism was needed to ensure management accountability. Corporations have a profound effect on the quality of our environment and our lives. If they were governed and operated more democratically, the influence they have on other social institutions such as government, education, and even the family could be expected to change in a positive direction.

The greatest and most significant divergence between the "American model" which is so widely recommended and the American reality is the separation of ownership and control. Conventional economies downplay the "separation of ownership and control into the agency problem of corporate governance" when there might be some divergence between the desires of the principles and the decisions of the agents.

Boards of Directors

http://www.mapnp.org/library/boards/brdrspon.htm

A board of directors is a group of people legally charged with the responsibility to govern a corporation. In a for-profit organization, the board is responsible to the stockholders. In a non-profit organization, the board reports to the stakeholders. The board of directors consist of many members, to include:

1. Board chair
2. Vice chair
3. Committee chair
4. Board member
5. Board secretary, and
6. Board treasurer.

Each of these members has their own duties to perform. New developments have led to the modern field of corporate governance which examines the legal, cultural and institutional arrangements that determine the direction and performance of corporations. Practitioners include: 1) the shareholders, who usually hold one vote per share of common stock owned; 2) the board members, whom shareholders elect, and 3) the management of the firm, which is usually headed by a CEO appointed by the board. Other participants include advisors, creditors, employees, customers, suppliers, government and its citizens. Each party can influence the firm's direction.

Ethical Considerations

http://www.mapnp.org/library/ethics/ethxgde.htm#anchor26548

Business ethics is knowing what is right or wrong in the workplace and attempting to do what is right-that is in regard to effects of products/services and in relationships with stakeholders. It becomes critical in the event of fundamental change. It is relatively simple to judge a business practice as ethically correct or incorrect. The hard part is understanding the concepts and techniques of ethical decision making so that you can reach better moral judgements. Many managers and theorists have turned to corporate social responsiveness, which studies how organizations become aware of and then respond to social issues. It takes two basic approaches. On the microlevel, it analyzes how individual companies respond to social issues. On the macro-level, it studies the forces that determine the social issues to which business should respond.

To engage in ethical reasoning, companies need to understand the ethical language, including the term's values, rights and duties, moral rules, and relationships. They must also understand the basic tenets of common morality, ranging from promise keeping to respect for property. To apply ethics, managers must weigh their opinions against the effects on different groups of stakeholders. To simplify this decision, managers can institutionalize ethics by creating corporate codes of conduct and ethics committees or by conduction ethics training programs and social audits.

Managers must also be aware of and avoid the temptations of naïve relativism, the idea that human beings are themselves the standard by which they should be judged, and cultural relativism, the idea that morality is relative to a particular culture. Relativism's main contribution to the debate on ethics in business is to remind us of the interplay between individuals and the community—a basic requirement for ethical thinking.

QUESTIONS

Separation of Ownership and Managerial Control
http://www.geocities.com/WallStreet/Floor/3935/j-firm.html
1. Describe the role of shareholder's in the standard Western model of a market economy as compared to a Japanese firm.

Boards of Directors
http://www.mapnp.org/library/boards/brdrspon.htm
2. List the major duties and responsibilities of the Board of Directors.

Ethical Considerations
http://www.mapnp.org/library/ethics/ethxgde.htm#anchor26548
3. Describe "business ethics." Give an overview of how a company would develop a code of ethics and how would they manage it effectively.

CHAPTER 12

Organizational Structure

An organizational structure defines how job tasks are formally divided, grouped and coordinated among its members. Each organization has its own structure that directly impacts its success. This chapter will examine the following: Forms of Structuring Organizations; The Effect of Structure on Strategy; and Structuring for International Operations.

Forms of Structuring Organizations
http://www.analytictech.com/mb021/orgtheory/htm

Classical theorists such as Taylor, Fayol and Weber believed that there is a single best way for an organization to be structured. However, each organization possesses various components that are unique. It is these components that determine the type of structure that is preferable to the organization. The following are some of the components that managers should consider when designing an organization's structure:

1. **Size**: this refers to capacity, number of personnel, outputs, and resources.
2. **Technology / Task**: it appears that certain activities correspond with certain structures. For example, companies that make one-of-a-kind custom products, or small quantities (unit production/small batch) have few levels of hierarchy.
3. **Environment**: this refers to an organization's ability to adapt to its environment, its dependence on its customers and suppliers, and the process of natural selection of those companies that are well suited to their environment.

Various forms of organizations include:

1. **Bureaucracy** (*http://www.analytictech.com/mb021/bureau.htm*). A form of organization that excels at businesses that are job specific and don't change quickly. There is centralized authority within a system of supervision and subordination. A bureaucracy functions by an extensive use of written documents.
2. **Departmentation / Departmentalization** (*http://analytictech.com/mb021/departme.htm*). The creation of a hierarchical system of supervision that utilizes small groups of workers that are supervised by coordinators or managers. There are common bases by which jobs are grouped for departmentation.
3. **Matrix Structure** (*http://www.analytictech.com/mb021/departme.htm*). A structure that creates dual lines of authority by combining two forms of departmentation: functional and product.
4. **Teams** (*http://www.analytictech.com/mb021/teamnotes.htm*). A group of workers that generate positive synergy through carefully coordinated efforts and goals. An increase in performance is expected through grouping those with complimentary skills and both individual and mutual accountability. Teams develop during predictable stages.

5. **Virtual / Network Organizations**
(*http://www.analytictech.com/mb021/virtual.htm*). An organization
that outsources its major business functions. A network of firms that
is held together by its product. This organization may not have a
permanent office.

The Effect of Structure on Strategy

An organization's structure is a means to help management to achieve
its objectives and mission. Strategy and structure are closely linked since
these objectives are derived from the organization's overall strategy. If
management makes significant changes in its organization's strategy, the
structure should also be modified to accommodate and support these
changes. Increasingly, companies are recognizing the critical effects of
organizational structure on their ability to compete and are moving to create the structure that they need. Organizational structure can positively
affect priorities related to quality, cost, service, and flexibility.

For a discussion of the importance of Organizational Structure in Total
Quality Management, see *http://www.skyenet.net/-leg/tqmodel/orgmenu.htm*.
Total Quality Management (TQM) focuses on product and process quality and supports the dual idea that quality is built in, not inspected in, and
that it is always cheaper to do it right the first time. An organization must
accurately account for both individual and team-process types of structure
if it is to produce a "balanced" TQM activity. All organizational TQM elements fall into one or more of the following three categories:
Organizational Structure; Product or Service Structure; and/or Marketing
Structure.

Structuring for International Operations

http://www.utc.edu/-eprater/Ops03/sld018.htm
http://www.analytictech.com/mb021/trends2.htm

The successful multinational company will structure its business to be globally integrated. Global integration means that a company manages all of its operations worldwide as a single entity or system in order to maximize a competitive advantage in both its domestic and international markets. This would include product development, purchasing, production, demand management and order fulfillment. The organizations that can develop new technologies faster, or can adapt to changes in the marketplace quicker, are the ones that will survive the competition. To maximize response time, organizations have been flattening, downsizing, and networking within their structures. Flat organizations make decisions quickly because each person is closer to the ultimate decision-makers. Horizontal communication among workers (networking) is encouraged. The flexibility of an organization to change with the market is a new way for businesses to do business.

QUESTIONS

Forms of Structuring Organizations
http://www.analytictech.com/mb021/orgtheory/htm
1. Briefly describe three factors that managers should consider when designing an organization's structure.

The Effect of Structure on Strategy
http://www.skyenet.net/-leg/tqmodel/orgmenu.htm
2. Name three categories in which the elements of TQM are included.

Structuring for International Operations

http://www.utc.edul-eprater/Ops03/sld018.htm
http://www.analytictech.com/mb021/trends2.htm

3. Describe the key benefit of global organizations.

http://www.analytictech.com/mb021/trends2.htm

4. List three current organizational trends and describe how they affect business in the 21st century.

CHAPTER 13

Corporate Innovation

Corporate innovation begins with leaders who have creative minds with new ideas. Those leaders need to create an environment where people contribute to improving the business by fostering new ways of thinking which create new knowledge, leading to new capacities and remarkable results.

Corporate innovation is what all of the following sub-topics are about. Entrepreneurship is an individual being innovative and starting his/her business, and intrapreneurship is an individual or group of individuals taking on the same concept except within the company. Which brings us to yet another innovation, buying innovations; mergers and acquisitions, a company as a whole venturing out to expand their company. One thing that each of these terms have in common is the ability to take risks, whether it is an individual, group of individuals or a company.

Entrepreneurship

http://www.babson.edu/entrep/outreach/ber98/2.htm
http://www.babson.edu/entrep/fer/papers95/hart.htm

Entrepreneurship is the process by which individuals pursue opportunities without regard to resources they currently control. By this definition, ownership or control of resources may not limit an entrepreneur's choice of opportunity. However, the resource choices that are necessarily made during the founding process may either limit or enhance the new venture's ability to succeed. This paper contends that founding resource choices have a significant impact on a new enterprise's viability and performance. It further argues that the founder(s)' industry-related experience can be a powerful proprietary resource that informs founding resource choices, thereby contributing to improved performance.

The entrepreneur's experience provides unique knowledge and reputation assets to the new enterprise. Experience-based knowledge, tacit and explicit, is linked to improved skills in resource specification, identification of appropriate resource providers, and development of selection criteria. Industry experience that establishes an entrepreneur's reputation contributes to success in attracting resource partners and in achieving favorable terms of cooperation.

The essence of entrepreneurship lies in one's creative base. Is it not true that successful entrepreneurs approach their business problems creatively? They become immersed if not obsessed with expressing their inner visions. Their approach to such unique expression is similar to that of an artist. As artists use tools such as paint, canvas, brushes, and vision, entrepreneurs use tools like capital, people, markets, and ideas. Entrepreneurs organize these familiar tools in fresh ways that give them a critical advantage in the business world.

Intrapreneurship

*http://entrepreneurs.about.com/smallbusiness/entrepreneurs/library/weekly/19
99/aa040999.htm*
*http://entrepreneurs.about.com/gi/dynamic/offsite.htm?site=http://intrapre-
neur.com/MainPages/History/IntraCorp.html*

At some point an entrepreneurial venture reaches the point of being an
established business. When that point is, is arguable. Some definitions
specify a certain dollar sales for a certain length of time, others say that
once the growth rate has leveled off, a business is no longer in its entrepreneurial stage. While reaching a point of "being there" is an achievement, a
real concern for most businesses is that somehow becoming an established
business means that the entrepreneurial spirit has been lost. Hence, the
growth of intrapreneurship—fostering entrepreneurism within established organizations.

The Intrapreneurial Organization. Pinchot in "Innovation Through
Intrapreneuring" credits intrapreneurs with increasing the speed and cost-
effectiveness of technology transfer from R&D to the marketplace. He
differentiates the intrapreneur from the inventor in the details they provide for their dreams. Both dream, but intrapreneurs are the "dreamers
who do"—they imagine in detail how to make their dream a marketplace
success. He also sees both intrapreneurs and entrepreneurs as not being
high-risk takers—50-50 odds are what they favor—not too easy and not
too hard—and within that framework they are constantly trying to
decrease the risk.

Three specific areas for entrepreneurial activity within the large corporation include:

1. Contracting out the sales of company products;
2. Performance-contracting within the corporation routine tasks, i.e., forming a group to sell a service to the corporation that the corporation would normally provide to itself;
3. Introducing a more entrepreneurial approach to the creation of new technology, new products, and new services.

To become an intrapreneur, an individual must risk something of value to himself. It may be just the time needed to complete the business plan and preliminary research while carrying out his normal duties. This is just one of the many steps it would take to becoming an intrapreneur.

Buying Innovations: Venture Capital

http://www.altosnet.com/EntrepreneurshipAtoZ/eaz41.1.htm

Business opportunities are everywhere for venture capitalists. Hundreds of business plans cross their desks every month, offering myriad opportunities. However, the successful venture capitalist invests in people first and business plans second.

When considering an investment opportunity, most venture capitalists look at the obvious trends and market niches. Transcending the business elements, however, the most important factor in a decision to invest in a company is the quality of the people. In real estate, the three biggest criteria are "location, location and location".

The venture capital axiom is people, people and people. Investors focus first on the management team's background. It is essential to understand its ability to deliver on its plan. In 20 years as a venture capitalist, I've picked enough winners and suffered through enough losers to develop my own measures.

Buying Innovations: Acquisitions

*http://entrepreneurs.about.com/gi/dynamic/offsite.htm?site=http://www.bvs%
2Dinc.com/developing%5Facquisition%5Fcriteria.htm*

You've made the decision: You want to buy a business. Before you go any further, it is essential to describe what you're looking for carefully enough so that your search efforts are well directed, but not so narrowly that you overlook qualified targets.

Rationale for Creating a Checklist for an Acquisition. To this end, you will want to define both the ideal and the essential characteristics of your target business. This definition gives those making the acquisition decision (the stockholders, professional advisors, board of directors, etc.) a common blueprint for finding and evaluating acquisition candidates. Developing a checklist of acquisition criteria can also reaffirm your goals or bring a part of your strategic plan more clearly into focus. You may also discover something about your business or goals you may not have known otherwise.

For example, let's assume one of your acquisition strategies is to acquire strong management. As you refine this objective you will probably become aware of previously unexamined strengths or weaknesses. You may realize a division head known for her rapport with clients also has strong team-building skills. As your advisors contact potential sellers, they will need to provide information about what you're looking for, along with a description of your company. The acquisition criteria you develop will form the core of this document.

QUESTIONS

Entrepreneurship
http://www.babson.edu/entrep/outreach/ber98/2.htm
1. What are the five qualities of essence?

Buying Innovations: Venture Capital
http://www.altosnet.com/EntrepreneurshipAtoZ/eaz41.1.htm
2. According to Jim Swartz, what are five traits, in order of importance, which investors (venture capitalist) look for in an entrepreneur?

Intrapreneurship
http://entrepreneurs.about.com/smallbusiness/entrepreneurs/library/weekly/1999/aa040999.htm
3. Describe the ten steps to an entrepreneurial organization.

CHAPTER 14

Strategic Management in Nonprofit Government Organizations

The concept of strategic planning and management determines where an organization is going in the future, how its going to get there, and how it will know if it got there or not. It involves the development of a vision or objective, a strategy to achieve that vision / objective, and an evaluation of that strategy. Major differences in how organizations carry out the various steps and associated activities in the strategic planning process / strategy, are more a matter of the size of the organization than its for-profit / nonprofit status. Small nonprofits and small for-profits tend to conduct somewhat similar planning activities that are different from those conducted in large organizations. On the other hand, large nonprofits and large for-profits tend to conduct somewhat similar planning activities that are different from those conducted in small organizations. The focus of the planning activities is often different between for-profits and nonprofits.

Nonprofits tend to focus more on matters of board development, fundraising and volunteer management. For-profits tend to focus more on activities to maximize profit. Nonprofit governmental organizations are compelled to achieve their objectives by law as stated in the Government Performance and Results Act (GPRA). This chapter will examine the following strategic management plans and objectives of the following nonprofit governmental organizations: Educational Institutions; Medical Organizations; and Governmental Agencies and Departments.

Educational Institutions

http://www.pen.k12.va.us/VDOE/Instruction/Govschools/
http://www.uscharterscholls.org/pub/uses docs/gi/overview.html
http://www.charterfriends.org/cfi-financing.html

Governor's schools are non-profit governmental educational institutions. The purpose of Governor's schools is to provide gifted students academic and visual and performing arts opportunities beyond those normally available in the students' home schools. Students are able to focus on a specific area of intellectual or artistic strength and interest and to study in a way that best suits the gifted learner's needs. Each program stresses non-traditional teaching and learning techniques. Governor's schools are administered by the state department of education, in cooperation with local school divisions, colleges and universities. Revenue for operation is provided by the state department of education and local school divisions.

Charter schools are also non-profit governmental educational institutions. A charter school is a public school, funded with public money and operated by parents, educators or community members. They must be approved by their local school district. Charter schools are non-sectarian public schools that operate free from many of the regulations that apply to traditional public schools. This deregulation is in exchange for a time-limited "charter" for student achievement. The "charter" that establishes each such school serves as a contract detailing the school's mission, program, goals, students served, methods of assessment, and ways to measure progress. The length of time for which charters are granted varies, but are usually granted for 3—5 years.

Both types of schools must be viewed from a strategic perspective in order to assure that they each contribute to the creation of the concept of value to the "customer", or in this case the parent—taxpayer. Each is also competing for the same tax dollars for funding as the other regular public schools. This is especially true for the charter schools as they run on per pupil allotment, hence public monies are supposed to follow the students directly to the charter school. Charter schools must be open to anyone, as they are considered "choice schools". Parents and students choose which school they would like to attend and are limited only by space availability. Each charter school must specify in its proposal how it will admit students. Most have adopted either a lottery or waiting list policy. Unlike charter schools, governor's schools have admissions tests and requirements. A school or division selection committee chooses from the nominees and forwards them to a state committee for selection.

It is clear that charter schools have more financing challenges (thus more strategic management challenges) than the other public educational institutions. Under their authorizing laws, charters lack the tax base and taxing authority that have traditionally financed public school facilities. Charter school operators also appear risky to traditional lenders because of their unproven records, limited terms, and dependence on choices made each year by students and their parents. New strategies are needed to allow charters access to the kind of lower-interest, tax-exempt, financing available to district public schools as well as equal access to general revenues, categorical grants, and other funding sources for traditional public school operations.

Medical Organizations
http://www.cdc.gov/irmo/strat97.html

There are a number of driving factors affecting the Centers for Disease Control's (CDC) plans for its public health mission of preventing disease, disability, and injury. Some of these are: health care reform, government wide staff reductions, the National Performance Review, and new legislation. There are also a number of global trends that provide opportunities for how CDC may achieve its goals through information technology such as the public/private telecommunications infrastructure investment and the convergence of communications media. The Information Resources Management (IRM) is a branch of the CDC which focuses on developing a national public health information infrastructure to ensure the health and well being of the American public. The following drive the strategic plan of the IRM:

1. Health Care Reform
2. National Performance Review
3. New Legislation
4. Government Wide Staff Reductions
5. Deficit Reduction

Governmental Agencies and Departments
http://aspe.hhs.gov/hhsplan/cappendix.html
http://www.mapnp.org/library/org-thry/np intro.html

The government agency called The Department of Health and Human Services has committed itself to achieve results that improve the lives of Americans; thus all of the strategic goals of HHS are programmatic goals. At the same time the Department recognizes that these goals will not be achieved without attention to the means that are employed to carry them out. HHS resolved to take full advantage of the tools that the Congress, the Executive Branch, and others have provided to improve the management and administration of HHS's program responsibilities. Some of these management tools are:

1. **The Government Performance and Results Act (GPRA)**—the principal tool that compels Federal programs to focus on results
2. **Chief Financial Officers Act (CFOA)**—assure financial accountability
3. **The Federal Acquisition Streamlining Act (FASA)**—broke new ground in acquisition methodology and embodies key principals of acquisition reform.

In line with the structure and diversity of the Department and its program activities, HHS management strategies have reflected a move away from a command and control leadership structure. Program legislation has compelled HHS components to operate as large, independent, and distinct agencies.

QUESTIONS

Educational Institutions
http://www.pen.k12.va.us/VDOE/Instruction/Govschools/
http://www.uscharterscholls.org/pub/uses docs/gi/overview.html
http://www.charterfriends.org/cfi-financing.html
1. Briefly describe the difference in Governor's Schools and Charter Schools and how their strategic management is similar.

Medical Organizations
http://www.cdc.gov/irmo/strat97.html
2. What is IRM and name four "drivers" of its strategic plan.

Governmental Agencies and Departments

http://aspe.hhs.gov/hhsplan/cappendix.html

http://www.mapnp.org/library/org-thry/np intro.html

3. Briefly describe three management tools provided by the government to assist its agencies in achieving their strategies / objectives.

CHAPTER 15

Knowledge Management

Knowledge is power in the business community. More and more educational conferences are being held on knowledge. In order to run a company appropriately, there must be a knowledge executive. The knowledge executive requires vision, creativity, and to be technology wise. There must also be a knowledge-based strategy. The knowledge-based strategy extends beyond executives to employees throughout the organization. Knowledge revolves heavily around technology. With the emergence of the Internet, knowledge is shared among many individuals, thereby creating virtual communities. Within the virtual communities, knowledge can be shared and increased. These exercises regarding knowledge management will cover three specific areas. They include the knowledge executive, knowledge-based strategy, and virtual communities. Knowledge management is important to the success of any business. By employing the three areas we will discuss, companies can gain advantages in the marketplace.

The Knowledge Executive

http://www.brint.com/wwwboard/messages/273.html

The knowledge executive has various characteristics, which include having a vision with the capability of developing and understanding the core of business issues the company is attempting to address and being aware of long term strategic and competitive needs of the company. The knowledge executive needs to have a good understanding of available technology and how they may be utilized within the company. The person should have an understanding of the human and cultural infrastructure that facilitates information sharing and facilitate the ongoing process of knowledge sharing and knowledge renewal. It is also important for them to be able to relate to the company's effectiveness criteria, given the current state of metrics of knowledge creation and measurement.

There should be an understanding of the cultural issues that are relevant to the knowledge creation process. The executive should be able to facilitate a "clan control" or "self control" based culture to facilitate dialog. They should have a good grasp of multiple perspectives on core issues and be willing to relate to diverse perspectives that are pertinent to the knowledge creation process. Being open-minded is essential, as well as, the willingness and ability to act as a liaison between the strategic needs of top management and operational concerns at the staff level.

The executive should possess a good understanding of various coordination and communication technologies, how they may be harnessed, and what factors are relevant to their application in group-level and organizational contexts. Finally, industry experience in business and technology issues, advanced [MBA or equivalent] education, exhibited capability or potential understanding for difference between data, information, and knowledge (pertinent to organizational strategic concerns) are necessary.

Knowledge-Based Strategy

http://www.fastcompany.com/online/02/stratsec.html

Winning depends on knowledge. Today knowledge is hot. Numerous conferences are being held on knowledge. We have now entered the knowledge economy. The following are five operating principles of knowledge:

1. Knowledge based strategy begins with strategy. A company must know the kind of value it wants to provide and who they would like to provide it to. After that it can link its knowledge resources to make a difference by serving customers around the world in a coordinated, consistent manner and respond quickly and effectively to changing competitive conditions. It can also offer its products or services to customers quicker, cheaper, effectively, and innovatively.

2. Knowledge-based strategies are only strategies if they are linked to traditional measures of performance. When knowledge cannot be connected to measurable improvements in performance, the knowledge revolution is short-lived. Knowledge has a clear impact on measures such as sales, costs, cycle time, productivity, and profitability. The point of knowledge-based strategy is to make money.

3. Executing a knowledge-based strategy is about nurturing people with knowledge. "Knowledge for knowledge's sake" lacks performance discipline. The trick is to balance the "hard" and the "soft"—tapping the knowledge locked in people's experiences. People are unwilling to share knowledge with their coworkers if the workplace culture is not supportive of learning, cooperation, and openness.

4. Organizations leverage knowledge through networks of people. Interconnectivity begins with people who are willing to connect. When successful, the combination of people and technology produces networks of people who transform themselves into "worknets," which are suborganizations or informal groups whose

collective knowledge accomplishes a specific task. The key to the worknet transition is that members must have compelling reasons for finding others with knowledge to share, who in turn have compelling reasons to share their knowledge when asked to do so.

5. People networks leverage knowledge through organizational "pull." The worker's need for help in solving business problems is the engine that drives knowledge development and sharing. The power is a result of the demand side rather than the supply side. The "pull-not-push" principle suggests problems should be framed and articulated specifically, therefore, knowledge-based strategies should emphasize on-the-job learning. "Just-in-time" learning takes place in the moment of actual need, creates the most value, and makes the biggest impression on the leaner and the organization. Learning is up to the individual. The essence of successful knowledge-based strategies is the company's capacity to raise the aspirations of each employee.

Virtual Communities

http://www.well.com/user/hlr/vcbook/vcbookintro.html

The principle of virtual communities is attempting to utilize the same rules in the world as we use in the community. The Internet is a perfect example of a virtual community. Daily there are conferences, personal contact, and business relations carried on over the World Wide Web, many times without the participants visualizing each other. The WELL (Whole Earth "Lectronic Link") is a computer conferencing system, which enables people to carry on public conversations from around the world via email. Basically, it is a community available via the computer. People in virtual communities utilize words on screens to exchange information, knowledge, brainstorm, gossip, conduct commerce, and many other uses. The U.S. senator who campaigned for many years to construct a National Research and Education Network that could host the virtual communities of the future is now vice president of the United States. The technology, which makes virtual communities possible, has the potential to bring enormous leverage to ordinary citizens at relatively low cost, which includes intellectual leverage, social leverage, commercial leverage, and political leverage. The CMC (computer-mediated communications)'s technical foundation is composed of computers and the switched telecommunications networks that carry telephone calls. It is predicted that when CMC technology becomes available to people anywhere, they will inevitably build virtual communities. Wide-area CMC networks that span continents and join thousands of smaller networks together are a spin-off of American military research. ARPANET was the first computer network and was created in the 1970's for the Department of Defense-sponsored researchers to operate different computers at a distance. Computer conferencing developed and became a tool for using the communication capacities of the networks to build social relationships across barriers of space and time. Programmers of ARPANET installed email features, since it was an easy thing to include. John Quarterman, in his book *The Matrix*, estimates there are nine hundred different worldwide networks today, excluding more than ten thousand already linked by the Internet "network of networks."

The Clinton administration took steps to amplify the Net's technical capabilities and availability via the National Research and Education Network. The High Performance, which was Al Gore's 1991 bill, was signed into law by President Bush and outlined Gore's vision for "highways of the mind" to be stimulated by federal research and development expenditures as a national intellectual resource and carried to the citizens by private enterprise. The ARPA (Advanced Research Projects Agency) venture was an example used by the Clinton-Gore administration from the 1960's and 1970's that produced the Net and the foundations of personal computing as an example of the way they see government and the private sector interacting in regard to future communications technologies. Telecommunication companies, television networks, computer companies, cable companies, and newspapers in the United States, Europe, and Japan in the private sector are jockeying for position in the nascent "home interactive information services industry." Millions of dollars are being invested by corporations in the infrastructure for new media in hopes it will earn billions of dollars. Marc Smith has been doing fieldwork in the WELL and the Net as a graduate student in sociology at the University of California at Los Angeles. He focuses on the concept of "collective goods." Every cooperative group of people exists in the face of a competitive world due to the group of people recognizing something valuable they can only gain from banning together. Smith proposes three kinds of collective goods as the social glue that binds WELL into something that resembles a community, which are social network capital, knowledge capital, and communication.

QUESTIONS

The Knowledge Executive
http://www.brint.com/wwwboard/messages/273.html
1. Briefly discuss the knowledge manager (executive) and his or her responsibility in relation to cultural issues.

Virtual Communities
http://www.well.com/user/hlr/vcbook/vcbookintro.html
2. Briefly discuss the Clinton-Gore administration's role in taking measures to amplify the Net's technical capabilities and its advancement.

Knowledge-Based Strategy
http://www.fastcompany.com/online/02/stratsec.html
3. List and describe three of the five operating principles of knowledge.

CHAPTER 16

Business Process Reengineering

In the business world today there is much talk of downsizing, rightsizing, reengineering, and other terms. There is a lot of focus on efficiency and productivity. Business process reengineering (BPR) stresses cost effectiveness, change, and employee involvement. It can discourage layoffs and job elimination by using attrition for decreased personnel requirements. Specific strategies are given for better utilization of BPR which addresses the customer, leader, and the company itself. Successful results of reengineering projects are achieved through common practices. These practices involve management support, methodology, business cases, and other success factors.

Overview of BPR

http://mijuno.larc.nasa.gov/dfc/bpre.html

Business Process Reengineering (BPR) is otherwise known as value engineering, which is applied to the system to bring forth, sustain, an retire the project. It has an emphasis on information flow. Utilizing BPR allows a company to identify low value functions and reduce costs. That enables the company to choose an alternative new and more cost-effective process that will implement the function of the current process to be developed. For BPR to be successful, management must initially make it clear to employees that the company will reinvest in them. If the commitment to lifelong employment cannot be made, management must use attrition for reduced personnel requirements. The people should not feel they are working themselves out of a job. BPR can be utilized to foster employee empowerment and teamwork under any TQM effort. BPR can bring about major internal and external quality increases, therefore, increasing value for the employee and the customer. The most important thing to remember from the competitive advantage perspective is to think about and to understand all outcomes before BPR is applied.

Strategic Management and BPR

http://www.prosci.com/future_IT.htm

There are various strategies recommended for CIOs (chief information officers) to adopt along three major themes:

1. Be customer-value driven. Develop a customer-driven business model and help align technology capabilities with business needs.
2. Be an innovation leader. Be a catalyst for the application of new technology and partner in business process improvement.
3. Create a standardized, open-systems environment and infrastructure that leverages common platforms to: (1) maximize speed and access to information; (2) allow flexibility and rapid development of specific end-user applications; and (3) streamline the integration of commercial and custom applications across the business.

Three roles were emphasized with regard to the future role of IT in business process reengineering, which include:

1. participate as a member of the reengineering team
2. define technology solutions to enable new business processes
3. implement technology needed to support new business processes

There are important activities or steps a CIO or IT manager can take to support a reengineering project:

1. Build solid relationships with operational managers and foster teamwork with IT staff and operational employees.
2. Develop a thorough understanding of the business strategy and help teams align technology solutions with the business direction and goals.
3. Be actively involved with the project team throughout the entire process.
4. Encourage early involvement of IT staff with the reengineering project.
5. Provide staff and resources needed to make the project successful
6. Facilitate clear communications and education across boundaries between IT and operations.

Best Practices
http://www.prosci.com/factors.htm

Over half of the early reengineering projects failed to be completed or to achieve bottom-line business results. Listed below are common success factors or themes, which lead to successful results for reengineering projects:

Top Management Sponsorship. Significant changes to processes, technology, job roles, or culture in the workplace requires resources, money, and leadership. Without the provision of strong and consistent support from top management, the money, resources, or leadership will be lacking over the life of the project and significantly decrease the chances of success.

Strategic Alignment. Reengineering project goals should be tied back to key business objectives and the main strategic direction for the organization. The linkage should show the connection from top to bottom and each person should easily connect the overall business direction with the reengineering effort. This alignment should be evidenced by financial performance, customer service, associate (employee) value, and the vision for the organization.

Compelling Business Case for Change, The business case must be able to be communicated in one page or less. Less is better. The project is not the only thing people have to do and the case must be made over and over throughout the project and during implementation. The simpler and shorter, the more understanding and compelling the case will be.

Proven Methodology. Methodology matters. Team members should understand reengineering and know how to go about it. An approach is needed that will meet the needs of the project and the team must understand and support it.

Effective Change Management. One must not forget the obstacle of resistance from those whom the implementers believe will benefit the most. Many projects underestimate the cultural impact of major processes and structural change. The result is not achieving the full potential of the change effort.

Line Ownership. The ultimate solution and results come back to the people who are accountable for day-to-day execution. Many teams are senior management responding to a crisis in line operations and often use external consultants or their own staff. It becomes a rescue operation. The terms of engagement and accountability must be clear. The line operation must have ownership. Those closest to the problem are often unable to see it. There is a lack of objectivity, external focus, technical re-design knowledge, and money. The positive side is the staff knows today's processes, the gaps and issues, and has the "front-line in-your-face" experience. Customers are also used to working with them. Expertise and objectivity is also needed from outside the organization.

Reengineering Team Composition. The team should be kept to fewer than ten players. Not every organization needs representation on the initial core team.

QUESTIONS

Overview of BPR
http://mijuno.larc.nasa.gov/dfc/bpre.html
1. List three disadvantages of business process reengineering (BPR).

Strategic Management and BPR
http://www.prosci.com/future_IT.htm
2. List the three major themes CIOs or heads of IT/IS departments should adopt strategies along.

Best Practices
http://www.prosci.com/factors.htm
3. Briefly discuss top management sponsorship in relation to BPR.

CHAPTER 17

The Turbulent Environment of Strategic Decision-Making

The environment of strategic-decision making goes from one extreme to the other. The turbulent environment of strategic decision making employs three aspects in this exercise. They include chaos theory and implications for strategic planning, complexity theory and implications for strategic management, and global scenarios for the future. The chaos theory is more on the qualitative level and encourages managerial planning for the future. The chaos theory divides strategic planning into four main classes. The complexity theory places more emphasis on employees and their natural ability to work together allowing the emergence of certain qualities. This theory is best compared to a flock of flying birds. Global scenarios for the future are explained based on the worlds in which they take place, including the market, fortress, and transformed worlds. Each of the three are explained in more detail later in the exercise. They deal with the new century globally in the past tense.

Chaos Theory and Implications for Strategic Planning

http://www.aom.pace.edu/bps/Papers/chaos.html

Chaos theory deals with "the qualitative study of unstable aperiodic behavior in deterministic nonlinear dynamical systems." In exploring the chaos theory, one must address a complex system. A complex system consists of a large number of agents interacting with each other in different ways. Managers are encouraged to strategically plan for the future. When that is not possible, they are encouraged to be adaptive and prepared to react to unexpected and unanticipated events. There are four class systems of behavior in cellular automata. The classes are involved in strategic planning. Class I models are a combination of live and dead cells quickly approaches a steady equilibrium state where all the cells are dead. Strategic planning in this system is a trivial case.

In Class II models, the cells develop into static groupings of live cells. The behavior of the system is stable and predictable. Strategic planning is relatively trivial. Planning is based on identifying repetitive historical patterns and projecting them into the future. Class III modes are chaotic. The cells alternate between "on" and "off" positions and there are no predictable patterns or stability. They display a sensitivity dependence on initial conditions, which cause accurate predictions for future conditions to be almost impossible. The Class IV model is a combination of Class I and Class II. It describes a coherent structure that propagated, grew, split apart, and recombined in a complex manner. Class IV models can produce "extended transients," which behave in a stable and predictable manner. There is also a degree of uncertainty. Extended transients in Class IV display predictable behavior for prolonged periods and make it seem that strategic planning is possible, however, planners should attempt a Stoic outlook on life.

Complexity Theory and Implications for Strategic Management

http://www.cio.com/archive/enterprise/041598_qanda_content.html

Complexity theory is best described as the behavior of a flock of birds. When the flock flies together they exhibit naturally emerging complex, unpredictable, creative behaviors from individual birds. When the flock flies in a v-formation, they are able to fly faster than an individual bird. The autonomous agents (birds) interact to form the flock and are known as a complex adaptive system. The birds must not bump into anything, keep up, and stay in close proximity to fly in a flock. When they follow those three rules, the birds become a cohesive, seemingly complicated group flying with speed and precision. Complexity theorists feel managers should allow creativity and efficiency to naturally emerge within the organization and to avoid imposing their own solutions on employees. This can be done by setting basic ground rules and encouraging interactions or relationships among employees so the solutions emerge from the bottom up. It is likely to unleash energy and enthusiasm from employees and managers cannot predict what the solutions (that the employees develop) will be. Complexity theory looks at the systems in organic, non-linear, and holistic ways.

Global Scenarios for the Future

http://mars3.gps.caltech.edu/whichworld//explore/scenarios.html

Global scenarios for the future are described in three ways, which include the market world, the fortress world, and the transformed world. These scenarios are taken from an insightful look into what the new century holds and presented as a "look back" on this century. These visions of the future are deliberately documented in optimistic tones.

Global scenario in the market world. Countries began to privatize, deregulate, rein in public spending, and unleash competitive market forces. They were joining the global market and dropping tariffs, promoting exports, and seeking foreign investment. Financial capital was being built up by encouraging savings and entrepreneurship. Human capital was built up by emphasizing education and health. Countries are creating modern infrastructures for transport and communications. The result of those changes produced a global economic boom of unprecedented breadth and longevity. Trade has grown twice as fast as economic output. The Free Trade Zone thrived *(http://mars3.gps.caltech.edu/whichworld//explore/scenarios/scenmw.html)*

Global scenario in the fortress world. Global scenario in the fortress world depicted an economic boom in the early decades with a decline in social and environmental areas. The living conditions in rural areas globally deteriorated. Along with the rapid economic growth there was worsening pollution to much of Asia and Latin America. There were deteriorating health conditions with increasing chronic lung disease in urban areas and epidemics of cancer from polluted waterways, as well as, virulent new diseases emerged from devastated forests and estuaries. There was an upsurge of violence and a growth of organized crime. Criminal organizations controlled the governments in several developing countries and elaborate computer crimes defrauded millions. A flood of illegal migrants poured into rich countries. Africa collapsed. Crime in Africa became the only way to feed a family and huge numbers fled across borders overwhelming stable countries. The industrial world turned inward and the world economy stagnated due to being faced with chronic instability.

Realistically today, incomes are lower than they were in 1980 in more than seventy countries. Pollution and other environmental problems are escalating. Water is scarce in North Africa and the Middle East. Malnutrition is widespread. Illegal migration is a large problem. Global criminal groups are outrunning national police efforts and an estimated five hundred billion dollars per year is spent in the drug business (*http://mars3.gps.caltech.edu/whichworld//explore/scenarios/scenfw.html*).

Global scenario in the transformed world. Global scenario in the transformed world predicted the anti-tobacco campaign in the United States was copied in other countries. Politicians called for a spirit of shared sacrifice. There was an agreement to cut emissions in half over a 30-year period by rationing through a licensing system the use of coal, oil, and natural gas and gradually raised the price of polluting fuels. The energy use dropped and gas-guzzling vehicles became socially unacceptable. New cars averaged one hundred miles per gallon and manufacturers could not keep up with production due to their popularity. Employment in Europe surged and labor costs decreased. There was a revolution in industrial efficiency increasing and recycling rates soured. There was a decline in consumer culture of the well-to-do countries, especially among young people with the outburst of low-impact life styles, vegetarian diets, and anti-materialistic ethics. Pollution and waste-disposal problems declined due to the need for less raw materials and energy. Codes of conduct were devised by coalitions of citizen's groups and industry representatives. There were dramatic social changes. The urban renaissance, which began as welfare reform, became a more sweeping transformation. More and more cities aimed at reducing crime, reviving its inner core, creating jobs, and reducing poverty, drug abuse, and other social problems. There were radical efforts to improve public education, create parks, and other environmental amenities. There was a religious revival and expansion of social ministry of virtually every denomination to aid the effort. The Church-related groups provided the cities with public funds to deliver social services, support stressed families, and motivate job seekers and recovering alcoholics.

Poverty declined and almost every social indicator showed improvement. Cities became attractive places to live and suburban areas' growth slowed. Global population peaked in 2040 and gradually declined afterwards (*http://mars3.gps.caltech.edu/whichworld//explore/scenarios/scentw.html*)

QUESTIONS

Chaos Theory and Implication for Strategic Planning
(*http://www.aom.pace.edu/bps/Papers/chaos.html*)
1. Briefly describe the four classes of behavior in cellular automata.

Global Scenarios for the Future
(*http://mars3.gps.caltech.edu/whichworld//explore/scenarios/scentw.html*)
1. Describe the predicted social changes for the new century in the global scenario: the transformed world.

Complexity Theory and Implications for Strategic Management
(*http://www.cio.com/archive/enterprise/041598_qanda_content.html*)
3 Describe the principles of the complexity theory and how they apply to strategic planning.

CHAPTER 18

Internet Enterprise Strategy and Design

Due to the increase in popularity of the Internet, more and more people are conducting business in a different manner. Companies are starting to use the Internet to advertise and sell their products. As a result of this, companies must design web sites so their customers can view their products. Business to Business has become a popular term used by those companies who conduct their business online. Also, adopting strategies such as CRM and ERP will help businesses benefit from the Internet.

Business to Business (B2B)

http://www.arthurandersen.com/resource2.nsf/AssetsByDescription/eB2Bresearchreport/$File/Financial.pdf

Electronic business to business (eB2B) is the bedrock of the new economy. The volume of transactions completely dwarfs that in the electronic business-to-consumer sector. eB2B represents 84% of total eBusiness revenue and the growth prospects are substantial. Revenues are predicted to be anywhere from $2.7 trillion to over $7 trillion within the next three years. As eB2B matures, it will offer the financial services industry a variety of strategies as well as challenges. eB2B solutions can position organizations for greater business profitability, efficiency and success.

Institutions are adopting a number of models in eB2B that can work. The choice of models must reflect the underlying business philosophy and market realities. Said another way, there are many unique solutions, and therefore, more than one way to be successful in this marketplace. 'eMarketplaces' using different models of buyer-seller relationships are expected to dominate online B2B trading and supply chain management.

The growth of eB2B relationships in the larger economy has been phenomenal. It is rewriting supplier-producer relationships in every industrial sector and driving efficiencies right across the production and distribution chain. To take advantage of this phenomenon, institutions are going to have to tackle a number of softer but no less strategically critical points. These include attracting and retaining the people who understand the new business models in a whole range of areas from technology through marketing.

Existing players rate themselves as tomorrow's winners despite the power eBusiness can give to new entrants. While the size and market clout of established institutions enable them to command disproportionate market resources and market space, maintaining industry leadership also demands the commitment of management to transform culture and strategy. New entrants will need to concentrate on their core competencies to understand where they can add value in an existing market. Many existing players will need to evaluate their position across the entire value chain.

Online B2B will provide the marketplace with real-time access to every component of the production and distribution chain, including its financing. The role of the financial institutions, especially those specializing in the transfer of cash, will consolidate, change or be eliminated entirely, depending on the type of marketplace that develops. To respond to the eBusiness challenge, financial services institutions are generally adopting one of three models. The first is to see the company's eBusiness platform as an extension of the existing brand without making significant changes to the underlying business. The second option takes this approach, but introduces structural changes to the underlying business. The third approach is to launch the eBusiness platform as an entirely new entity, incorporating a different business model from the core business, as well as a different brand.

Enterprise Resource Planning (ERP)

http://www.itworks.be/ERP/index.html

In the past decade the business environment has changed dramatically. The world has become a small and very dynamic marketplace. Organizations today confront new markets, new competition and increasing customer expectations. This has put a tremendous demand on manufacturers to:

1. Lower total costs in the complete supply chain;
2. Shorten throughout times;
3. Reduce stock to a minimum;
4. Enlarge product assortment;
5. Improve product quality;
6. Provide more reliable delivery dates and higher service to the customer;
7. Efficiently coordinate global demand, supply, & production.

Thus today's organizations have to constantly re-engineer their business practices and procedures to be more responsive to customers and competition. To help with this re-engineering process, the tool, enterprise resource planning (ERP), is used.

Enterprise Resource Planning comes from the term MRP-II (Manufacturing Resources Planning). In the 1980's, the concept of MRP-II evolved which was an extension of MRP to shop floor and distribution management activities. In the early 1990's, MRP-II was further extended to cover areas like Engineering, Finance, Human Resources, Projects Management, etc. the complete gamut of activities within any business enterprise. Hence, the term ERP was coined.

ERP is a software infrastructure that helps to manage the different parts of a company or business. The goal is to create a complete integration of systems across the departments in a company as well as across the enterprise as a whole. ERP integrates databases, applications, interfaces, tools, & BPR. ERP prevents people from within the company from doing the same thing twice, makes sure you have the right things in stock at the right time, & helps you satisfy the needs of customers.

Customer Relationship Management (CRM)

http://menconi.CRMproject.com

A CRM strategy means that operations revolve around the customer and involve much more than installing any one application, embracing a new technology, or even committing to one vendor's CRM suite. It sparks new ways of doing business and provides better insight into customer behavior. CRM strategies require a cultural shift that aligns a company, its employees, and its systems toward customers and away from traditional product or process centric models.

CRM is a strategy that is used in competitive environments that combines the information, systems, policies, processes, and employees of an enterprise in an effort to attract and retain profitable customers. CRM applications and technologies are tools used to implement such a strategy and must be woven into the fabric of a company's business strategy, not bolted on to it.

When developing a CRM strategy, it must come from the top. CRM is an all-encompassing strategy, and no one department, call center, or Information Technology (IT) manager can drive the cross-functional process changes required. A recent study showed CEOs were directly involved in successful CRM initiatives more than 40% of the time. A great CRM strategy:

1. Realigns and reinvents business processes
   a. Requires policy decisions that effect the online organization
   b. Opens the enterprise for customer self-sale and self-service
2. Is based upon the full range of technology
   a. Enables new business strategies
   b. Streamlines processes and speeds communication
   c. Adapts quickly to support business changes
3. Provides a complete view of each customer
4. Uses technology to make the most of each customer contact
   a. Each contact becomes an opportunity to sell
   b. Customers can use seller's processes instead of building their own
5. Puts current applications to strategic use
   a. Data warehouse stores used to strategic advantages
   b. Back-office system integrated for customer support
6. Drives ROI for both users and customers

CRM strategies result in increased sales, new ways to differentiate in the marketplace, the ability to absorb new business methods such as the Internet, and other benefits.

QUESTIONS

Enterprise Resource Planning (ERP)
http://www.itworks.be/ERP/index.html
1. List the five items that were discussed in the paper that ERP integrates.

Business to Business
http://www.arthurandersen.com/resource2.nsf/AssetsByDescription/eB2Br esearchreport/$File/Financial.pdf
2. List the three models that financial services institutions are adopting as a result of the growth of B2B.

Customer Relationship Management (CRM)
http://menconi.CRMproject.com
3. Discuss the six steps that a great CRM strategy must have.

CHAPTER 19

Finance and Budgeting Basics for Strategic Management

Business strategy decisions call for managers to be knowledgeable in many areas, including finance and budgeting. By being familiar with these two areas, it will help the company set important guidelines for which it will base its business strategies. Managers must constantly evaluate the financial performance of their business. Financial measures can be used to help assess the current situation of the company as well as past situations. One way managers can evaluate their financial performance is by using financial ratio analysis. It is also important for managers to be able to financially and strategically plan for their business so that the business knows its direction and objectives.

Evaluating Financial Performance

*http://209.241.14.8/fmpro?-db=homepage.fp5&-format=fulltext1.htm
&Record=6335&-find*

Many small and mid-sized companies are run by entrepreneurs who are highly skilled in some key aspect of their business-perhaps technology, marketing or sales-but are less savvy in financial matters. There are some powerful and widely used tools for analyzing the financial health of a company which are not very difficult to calculate or very complicated to use. These tools, known as ratios, will help to turn the raw data that are in the financial statements into information that will be useful in running the business. Financial ratios measure your company's productivity. There are many ratios you can use, but they all measure how good a job your company is doing in using its assets, generating profits from each dollar of sales, turning over inventory, or whatever aspect of your company's operation that you are evaluating.

Financial ratio analysis is nothing more than simple comparisons between specific pieces of information pulled from your company's balance sheet and income statement. Financial ratio analysis can be used in two different but equally useful ways. You can use them to examine the current performance of your company in comparison to past periods of time, from the prior quarter to years ago. Even better, it can direct your attention to potential problems that can be avoided. In addition, you can use these ratios to compare the performance of your company against that of your competitors or other members of your industry. The following are four types of ratios: Common size; Liquidity; Efficiency; and Solvency.

Common size ratios can be developed from both balance sheet and income statement items. The phrase "common size ratio" may be unfamiliar to you, but it is simple in concept and just as simple to create. You just calculate each line item on the statement as a percentage of the total. For example, each of the items on the income statement would be calculated as a percentage of total sales. Similarly, items on the balance sheet would be calculated as percentages of total assets (or total liabilities plus owner's equity). Common size ratios are a simple but powerful way to learn more about your business. They allow you to make knowledgeable comparisons with past financial statements for your own company and to assess trends in your financial statements.

Liquidity ratios measure your company's ability to cover its expenses. The two most common liquidity ratios are the current ratio and the quick ratio. The current ratio answers the questions, "Does the business have enough current assets to meet the payment schedule of current liabilities, with a margin of safety?" It is computed by dividing total current assets by total current liabilities. The quick ratio tests whether a business can meet its obligations even if adverse conditions occur. The formula for the quick ratio is current assets less inventory divided by current liabilities.

Operating ratios help to measure the efficiency of the company's operations. The four ratios that are most widely used are the inventory turnover ratio, sales to receivables ratio, days' receivables ratio, and return on assets.

Solvency ratios measure the stability of a company and its ability to repay debt. They give a strong indication of the financial health and viability of your business. The following are solvency ratios:

1. Debt-to-worth ratio
2. Working capital
3. Net sales to working capital
4. Z-score

Financial ratio analysis is one way to turn financial statements, with their long columns of numbers, into powerful business tools. Financial ratio analysis offer a simple solution to numbers overload.

Financial Planning and Forecasting
http://www.exinfm.com/training/

Financial planning and forecasting are tools used by managers when making strategic decisions. Strategic planning is a process in which goals and objectives are established over a long period of time. This process can result in financial implications which means the creation and implementation of budgets. Financial planning starts at the top of the organization however, it is very important for businesses to have learning take place at all levels of the organization.

Financial planning is a continuous process of directing and allocating financial resources to meet strategic goals and objectives. The detail budgets are included in the Operating Plan. The Operating Plan is a Plan of Action which helps to implement the Strategic Plan. The Master Budget can be broken down into the Operating Plan and the Financial Plan. The Operating Plan consists of the Sales Forecast, Budgeted Production, Budgeted Production Costs, Budgeted Cost of Goods Sold, Budgeted Operating Expenses, and Budgeted Income Statement. The Financial Plan consists of Budgeted Retained Earnings, Budgeted Capital Expenditures, Change in Fixed Assets, Budgeted Balance Sheet, and the Cash Budget.

A forecasting approach relies on past relationships and existing historical information. Forecasting helps to make better decisions. Two types of forecasting techniques are quantitative and qualitative. Other approaches to forecasting are exponential smoothing, regression analysis, sensitivity analysis, or financial models.

Strategic Planning

http://www.planware.org/strategy.htm

Senior business managers are often so preoccupied with immediate issues that they lose sight of their ultimate objectives. That's why a business review or preparation of a strategic plan is a virtual necessity. This may not be a recipe for success, but without it a business is much more likely to fail. A sound plan should:

1. Serve as a framework for decisions or for securing support/approval.
2. Explain the business to others in order to inform, motivate & involve.
3. Assist benchmarking and performance monitoring.
4. Stimulate change and become a building block for the next plan.

A strategic plan should not be confused with a business plan. A strategic plan is likely to be a very short document whereas a business plan is likely to be much more substantial and detailed. When creating a strategic plan, it should be visionary, conceptual and directional as well as realistic and attainable to allow the planner to think strategically and act operationally.

As the precursor to developing a strategic plan, it is desirable to clearly identify the current status, objectives and strategies of an existing business or the latest thinking in respect of a new venture. Correctly defined, these can be used as the basis for a critical examination to probe existing or perceived strengths, weaknesses, threats and opportunities. This then leads to strategy development covering the following issues: vision, mission, objectives, values, strategies, goals and programs.

Most managers will find it exceedingly difficult to develop a future strategy for a business without knowing its current strategies and measuring their success to date. The starting point must be to determine a company's existing vision, mission, objectives and strategies. Then judge these against actual performance along the following lines:

1. Is the current vision being realized?
2. How has the company's mission and objectives changed over the past say, three years? Why have the changes occurred or why have no changes occurred? Identify primary reasons and categories as either internal or external.
3. Describe the actual strategies followed over the past few years.
4. Critically examine each strategy statement by reference to activities and actions in key functional areas covering such matters as:
5. How has the company been managed?
6. How has the company been funded?
7. How has the company sought to increase sales and market share?
8. How has productivity/costs moved?

After reviewing the firm's past aims and achievements, the SWOT analysis can be used. Strengths and weaknesses are essentially internal to the organization and relate to matters concerning resources, programs and organization in key areas. Threats and opportunities are essentially external to the organization. Once the SWOT review is complete, the future strategy may be readily apparent or, as is more likely the case, a series of strategies or combinations of tactics will suggest themselves. Use the SWOT analysis to help identify possible strategies as follows:

1. Build on strengths
2. Resolve weaknesses
3. Exploit opportunities
4. Avoid threats

The resulting strategies can then be filtered and molded to form the basis of a realistic strategic plan.

QUESTIONS

Strategic Planning
http://www.planware.org/strategy.htm
1. List the four attributes a strategic plan should have.

Financial Planning and Forecasting
http://www.exinfm.com/training/
2. List six types of forecasting techniques.

Evaluating Financial Performance
http://209.241.14.8/fmpro?-db=homepage.fp5&-format=fulltext1.htm&Record=6335&-find
3. Explain why using financial ratio analysis is important.

CHAPTER 20

Organizational Learning as Strategy

Organizational learning has become an important strategy for businesses. The advantage gained from learning is that the organization's employees are able to respond quickly and effectively to certain events as well as being able to satisfy customers' needs with new products and improved services.

Basic concepts

http://learning.mit.edu/res/wp/learning_sys.html

With the decline of some well-established firms, the diminishing competitive power of many companies in a burgeoning world market, & the need for organizational renewal and transformation, interest in organizational learning has grown. Senior managers in many organizations are convinced of the importance of improving learning in their organizations.

Organizational learning can be defined as the capacity or processes within an organization to maintain or improve performance based on experience. Learning is a systems-level phenomenon because it stays within the organization, even if individuals change. For an organization, learning is as much a task as the production and delivery of goods and services.

Three factors identify some of the qualities of an effective learning organization that diligently pursues a constantly enhanced knowledge base. Those three factors are:

1. Well-developed core competencies that serve as launch points for new products and services.
2. An attitude that supports continuous improvement in the business's value-added chain.
3. The ability to fundamentally renew or revitalize.

Based on these factors, several assumptions can be made. The first is that an organization's ability to survive and grow is based on advantages that stem from core competencies that represent collective learning. Another assumption is that the value chain of any organization is a domain of integrated learning. The last assumption is that the learning process has three identifiable stages. They are knowledge acquisition, knowledge sharing, and knowledge utilization. These three stages consist of seven learning objectives and ten facilitating factors.

Learning may take place in planned or informal ways. There are strategies for improving organizational learning capabilities. The first is to focus on a single stage of the learning cycle. The second is to select an option for focus whether it's improving on learning orientations or it's changing both learning orientations and facilitating factors. It is one thing to develop a plan for improving what is already done reasonably well; it is another to engage in nothing less than near-total transformation. It is one thing to stay within accepted, assimilated paradigms; it is another to replace institutionalized models.

The Role of Learning in Strategic Management
http://www.geocities.com/Athens/Acropolis/1002/learning.html

Learning can help businesses facilitate the strategy process. It is very important for businesses to have learning take place at all levels of the organization. Learning is a skill we all possess intrinsically and that is used throughout our lives. It is now widely believed that organizational learning can significantly improve corporate performance and this has spurned an industry of writings from operational researchers, planners, etc., and international conferences to aid in the transmission of this new-found knowledge.

The two basic forms of learning are habit forming and active. Habit forming takes place when the learner is conditioned to react in a certain way. Active learning is done through experiments. Effective learning makes one better able to cope with problems.

Strategy planning starts by examining the interactions between the organization and its environment. Strategy can be perceived as the following:

1. A game plan
2. A threat
3. A pattern of behavior
4. A position in the marketplace
5. A perspective shared by members of an organization

Managers, who want to be strategic, will need to be able to change their views as the world changes. The quicker the manager is able to react to changes, the more successful they will be.

The Meta-Strategic Cycle
http://www.mcb.co.uk/services/articles/liblink/tlo/limerick.htm

The meta-strategic cycle's theory is that change takes place at different levels within an organization, from superficial systems of action to change in the very identity of the organization. This concept helps to explore the differences between the thoughts of the transformational theorists and the learning organization theorists. The meta-strategic cycle links together the concepts of identity, vision, organizational action, and configuration.

Vision is the image a leader has on where they want the organization to be in the future. The vision can vary from a leader's dream, a mission statement of the organization, or a goal. The vision helps to establish the identity of the organization. The identity image defies logic within the organization and it also gives legitimacy and continuity to action. The identity image is capable of change throughout the long term. Effective strategic managers do attempt to make this image more concrete and accessible, often by writing it down in the credo, philosophy, or mission statement. The identity image consists of the organization's values and a continuing vision of the potential of the organization. The configuration design brings together a desired strategy, structure and culture of the organization into a coherent whole.

QUESTIONS

The Meta-Strategic Cycle
http://www.mcb.co.uk/services/articles/liblink/tlo/limerick.htm
1. List the 4 concepts which are linked by the meta-strategic cycle.

The Role of Learning in Strategic Management
http://www.geocities.com/Athen/Acropolis/1002/learning.html
2. List the 5 perceptions of strategies.

http://learning.mit.edu/res/wp/learning_sys.html
3. List the three factors which identify the qualities of an effective learning organization that diligently pursues a constantly enhanced knowledge base and the assumptions which can be made.

About the Author

Brian Satterlee, who holds doctorates in Education and in Business Administration, is active in three fields: individual, corporate and education.

- In the corporate field, he has served as an organizational consultant specializing in performance improvement.
- In the field of education, he has served as full professor of Business Administration at three private liberal arts universities. He has been teaching college-level courses continuously since 1980.
- Finally, he has served as a professional coach, helping people worldwide achieve their dreams and goals.

Leadership positions included School of Business Dean, Dean of Graduate and Professional Studies, Dean of Adult Education, Business Department Chairperson, Director of Technical Education, and Division of Engineering Technology Chairperson.

He has served on many reaffirmation of accreditation teams for the Southern Association of Colleges and Schools, and has experiences consulting with organizations in the Caribbean Basin concerning program review, evaluation, and strategic planning. He has published nationally within his discipline, and has presented papers at professional conferences.

Dr. Satterlee has consulted with numerous organizations on topics related to strategic management and planning, human resources development, distance learning initiatives, leadership, and the development and evaluation of educational programs and services.

Brian Satterlee may be reached at

www.maxpages.com/catalyst

Appendix

ANSWERS TO THE END OF CHAPTER QUESTIONS

CHAPTER 1 ANSWERS

1. The first set of choices relate to the objectives that the firm is trying to achieve: (1) Selection of Goals: What goals does the company seek to achieve? What is the "mission" of the firm? (2) Market Positioning: Where is the firm currently? Where should it be to achieve its goals? How does it get there?

2. (A) Knowledge generated by the firm through its own R&D efforts, and translated into innovation; (B) Knowledge purchased by the firm. This could be disembodied in the form of technology licenses, patents etc., or embodied in the inputs the firm purchases. Technology licenses and inputs can be purchased either locally or from a foreign source. Thus, technology can be acquired through domestic or foreign inputs. (C) Technology spillovers created by knowledge generated by other organizations. It can be created from knowledge generated from domestic agencies such as firms, government, private research institutions, individual researchers, and knowledge generated abroad.

3. (A) Attempt to attain a higher degree of competitive advantage in existing products; (B) Improve resource planning by introducing "just in time" techniques and coordinating more closely with marketing; (C) Improve market intelligence and increase economic analysis; (D) Introduce more rigorous control systems to monitor company performance; (E) Communicate company goals to everyone; develop a company culture so that individuals can identify with the company's objectives.

CHAPTER 2 ANSWERS

1. The organization's goals, objectives and strategies by which it plans to achieve its vision, mission and values

2. Individuals who have stake in or an effect on a business.

3. A good strategic plan should:
   a. Serve as a framework for decisions or for securing support/approval.
   b. Explain the business to others in order to inform, motivate & involve.
   c. Assist benchmarking & performance monitoring.
   d. Stimulate change and become building block for next plan

CHAPTER 3 ANSWERS

1. What obstacles do you face? What is your competition doing? Are the required specifications for your job, products or services changing? Is

changing technology threatening your position? Do you have bad debt or cash-flow problems?

2. First, no participant is told the identity of the other members of the group, which is easily accomplished if, as is common, the forecasts are obtained by means of questionnaires or individual interviews. Second, no single opinion, forecast, or other key input is attributed to the individual who provided it or to anyone else. Third, the results from the initial round of forecasting must be collated and summarized by an intermediary (the experimenter), who feeds these data back to all participants and invites each to rethink his or her original answers in light of the responses from the group as a whole. Fourth, the process of eliciting judgments and estimates should be continued until either of two things happens: The consensus within the group is close enough for practical purposes, or the reasons why such a consensus cannot be achieved have been documented.

3. **Economic conditions**—which deals with the general state of the economy in terms of inflation, income levels, gross domestic product, unemployment, and other related indicators of economic health; **Socio-cultural conditions**—the state of prevailing social values on such matters as human rights and environment, trends in education and related social institutions, as well as demographic patterns; **Legal-political conditions**—general state of philosophy and objectives of political parties running the government, as well as laws and government regulations; **Technological conditions**—general state of the development and availability of technology in the environment, including scientific advancements; **Natural environment conditions**—general state and nature and conditions of the natural or physical environment.

CHAPTER 4 ANSWERS

1. The deterrents faced by members of one strategic group to enter and compete in another strategic group within the industry.

2. Collecting the information; Converting the information into intelligence; Communicating the intelligence; Countering any adverse competitor actions

3. The threat of new entrants; The bargaining power of suppliers; Threats from substitute products or services; The bargaining power of buyers; Rivalry amongst existing firms

CHAPTER 5 ANSWERS

1. Core capabilities include vision, understanding, and thinking in wholes.

2. Benefits of value-chain analysis are:
   a. It is a powerful resource used to diagnose and strengthen competitive advantage.
   b. It focuses on value-adding business activities.
   c. It breaks down an enterprise into parts and helps in adopting a technology that will increase the overall profit.

3. Outsourcing serves as a central management tool in redefining organizations. It is a key factor for companies to successfully compete in the global economy. Outsourcing is more than purchasing, and it is more than consulting. It is a long-term results-oriented

relationship for a whole business activity over which the provider has a large amount of control and managerial discretion. Outsourcing is the use of outside business relationships to perform necessary business activities and processes in lieu of internal capabilities. Outsourcing also acts as a communication link between the user and provider in which both work together to explain the services that are delivered.

CHAPTER 6 ANSWERS

1. Organizational customers are broken down into: user customers, original-equipment manufacturers, and resellers.

2. Four steps to help satisfy customer needs are: recognize your organization's need for a customer service plan; determine the level of service needed; establish goals for the plan for what you want to accomplish; Adjust the plan accordingly when new information is learned.

3. Develop a service vision in what you want your company to represent. Recognize and reward employees who outperform stated customer satisfaction objectives and goals, and those who make recommendations on how to handle customer complaints better, how to be more effective, or who consistently offers better policies and procedures. Hold regular "customer satisfaction" meetings and ask employees what else they recommend doing to increase customer satisfaction and establish stronger loyalty from customers. Focus groups are also a popular method to gather customer information.

CHAPTER 7 ANSWERS

1. Advantages of related diversification are it allows firm to maintain unity in business activities, takes advantage of a firm in what it does best, helps achieve economies of scope.

2. Restructurings often include an overabundance of items including the costs of employee severance and termination, costs to eliminate or curtail product lines, costs to consolidate or relocate operations, costs for new systems development or acquisition, losses relating to asset impairments, and losses on disposal of assets.

3. In a merger, one company may purchase all or part of another; two companies may merge by exchanging shares; or a wholly new company may be formed through consolidation of the old companies. The basic requirements for the success of a merger are that it fit into a soundly conceived long-range plan and that the resulting firm has performance characteristics superior to those attainable by the previous companies independently.

CHAPTER 8 ANSWERS

1. Four strengths of low-cost leadership are:
   1. it puts a company in position to use low prices as a defense against substitutes.
   2. it provides protection from bargaining leverage of powerful buyers.
   3. it provides protection from bargaining leverage of powerful suppliers.

4. it allows a better position than rival competitors to compete offensively on basic of price.

2. Four reasons that make a differentiation strategy fail are:
   1. failing to signal value.
   2. not understanding what buyers want.
   3. charging a price premium.
   4. over-differentiating.

3. Focus strategy works best when no other rivals are concentrating on the same segment and when firm resources do not allow it to go after a larger piece of the market. Also, it works best when industries have many different segments that will create more focused opportunities. One of the risks involved in this strategy is competitors find effective ways to match a focuser's capabilities in serving niche. Another risk is the segment becomes so attractive that it becomes crowded with rivals.

CHAPTER 9 ANSWERS

1. Strategic alliances are partnerships between firms who combine their resources, capabilities, and core competencies in order to pursue mutual interests.

2. Competition reduction strategies can become illegal when firms use price fixing.

3. Network Strategies are actions taken to increase the quality and quantity of business through networking. Networking is a tool that lets departments share information allowing the company to act as one.

4. Network strategies help to improve business by lowering costs and increasing efficiency and communication.

5. There are four goals of strategic alliances. The first is to gain market power. The second is to gain access to the markets along with ideas and materials. The third and forth is to speed up development or entry into a market and share risk of new products. They are meant for companies to combine resources to pursue similar interests

CHAPTER 10 ANSWERS

1. Globalization

2. A start up investment in new facilities in a foreign market

3. Go to URL: *http://nikebiz.com/community/index.shtml* & visit their global facts page to discuss Nike's involvement in the global community. Examples of response include:

   Nike provides new world class, environmentally friendly outdoor sports facility for the kids of South Sydney What do you get when you combine 2,000 car tires and 12,000 recycled athletic shoes…a world class outdoor sports facility for the kids of South Sydney!

Nike sponsored the *YWCA—Race Against Racism* with a $75,000 grant in Washington, DC on April 29, 2000. The Race is a tremendous opportunity to raise awareness, eliminate racial barriers and celebrate.

Nike Thailand Wins the "**Human Development Center Good Samaritan Award.**"

CHAPTER 11 ANSWERS

1. In the standard Western model of a market economy, market relationships between buyers and sellers are thought of as spot or auction market transactions. If the same commodity can be purchased from another seller at a lower price, then demand switches to the lower-cost supplier. In the Japanese economy, there is the rather different notion of relational contracting (see Goldberg 1980). It is a long-term high-trust relationship with extensive communication along many other dimensions than just price and quantity. Relational contracting extends well outside the specific *keiretsu* groupings. Contractual partners might exchange shares as a symbol of the long-term relationship. In the Western model, shareholding is by itself a relationship; it makes the shareholder an "owner" of the company. If the shareholder has some other business relationship with the company, that is considered a "conflict of interest." In the Japanese firm, the shareholders are not sovereign. In the

Japanese model, shareholding is usually symbolic of some other business relationship.

2. Major duties include:

Provide continuity for the organization by setting up a corporation or legal existence, and to represent the organization's point of view through interpretation of its products and services, and advocacy for them

Select and appoint a chief executive to whom responsibility for the administration of the organization is delegated, including:

- to review and evaluate his/her performance regularly on the basis of a specific job description, including executive relations with the board, leadership in the organization, in program planning and implementation, and in management of the organization and its personnel

- to offer administrative guidance and determine whether to retain or dismiss the executive

Govern the organization by broad policies and objectives, formulated and agreed upon by the chief executive and employees, including to assign priorities and ensure the organization's capacity to carry out programs by continually reviewing its work

Acquire sufficient resources for the organization's operations and to finance the products and services adequately

Account to the public for the products and services of the organization and expenditures of its funds, including:

- to provide for fiscal accountability, approve the budget, and formulate policies related to contracts from public or private resources

- to accept responsibility for all conditions and policies attached to new, innovative, or experimental programs.

Major responsibilities include:
Determine the Organization's Mission and Purpose
Select the Executive
Support the Executive and Review His or Her Performance
Ensure Effective Organizational Planning
Ensure Adequate Resources
Manage Resources Effectively
Determine and Monitor the Organization's Programs and Services
Enhance the Organization's Public Image
Serve as a Court of Appeal
Assess Its Own Performance

3. Business ethics is knowing what it right or wrong in the workplace and doing what's right—this is in regard to effects of products/services and in relationships with stakeholders. The following list describes various types of benefits from managing ethics in the workplace.

Attention to business ethics has substantially improved society. A matter of decades ago, children in our country worked 16-hour days. Workers' limbs were torn off and disabled workers were condemned to poverty and often to starvation. Trusts controlled some markets to the extent that prices were fixed and small businesses choked out. Price fixing crippled normal market forces. Employees were terminated based on personalities. Influence was applied through intimidation and harassment. Then society reacted and demanded that businesses place high value on fairness and equal rights. Anti-trust laws were instituted. Government agencies were established. Unions were organized. Laws and regulations were established.

Ethics programs help maintain a moral course in turbulent times. Attention to business ethics is critical during times of fundamental change—times much like those faced now by businesses, both non-profit or for-profit. During times of change, there is often no clear moral compass to guide leaders through complex conflicts about what is right or wrong. Continuing attention to ethics in the workplace sensitizes leaders and staff to how they want to act—consistently.

Ethics programs cultivate strong teamwork and productivity. Ethics programs align employee behaviors with those top priority ethical values preferred by leaders of the organization. Ongoing attention and dialogue regarding values in the workplace builds openness, integrity and community—critical ingredients of strong teams in the workplace. Employees feel strong alignment between their values and those of the organization. They react with strong motivation and performance.

Ethics programs support employee growth and meaning. Attention to ethics in the workplace helps employees face reality, both good and bad—in the organization and themselves. Employees feel full confidence they can admit and deal with whatever comes their way.

Ethics programs are an insurance policy—they help ensure that policies are legal. There is an increasing number of lawsuits in regard to personnel matters and to effects of an organization's services or products on stakeholders. As mentioned earlier in this document, ethical principles are often state-of-the-art legal matters. These principles are often applied to current, major ethical issues to become legislation. Attention to ethics ensures highly ethical policies and procedures in the workplace. It's far better to incur the cost of mechanisms to ensure ethical practices now than to incur costs of litigation later. A major intent of well-designed personnel policies is to ensure ethical treatment of employees, e.g., in matters of hiring, evaluating, disciplining, firing, etc.

Ethics programs help avoid criminal acts "of omission" and can lower fines. Ethics programs tend to detect ethical issues and violations early on so they can be reported or addressed. In some cases, when an organization is aware of an actual or potential violation and does not report it to the appropriate authorities, this can be considered a criminal act, e.g., in business dealings with certain government agencies, such as the Defense Department. The recent Federal Sentencing Guidelines specify major penalties for various types of major ethics violations. However, the guidelines potentially lowers fines if an organization has clearly made an effort to operate ethically.

Ethics programs help manage values associated with quality management, strategic planning and diversity management—this benefit needs far more attention. Ethics programs identify preferred values and ensuring organizational behaviors are aligned with those values. This effort includes recording the values, developing policies and procedures to align behaviors with preferred values, and then training all personnel about the policies and procedures. This overall effort is very useful for several other programs in the workplace that require behaviors to be aligned with values, including quality management, strategic planning and diversity management. Total Quality Management includes high priority on certain operating values, e.g., trust among stakeholders, performance, reliability, measurement, and feedback. Eastman and Polaroid use ethics tools in their quality programs to ensure integrity in their relationships with stakeholders. Ethics management techniques are highly useful for managing strategic values, e.g., expand market share, reduce costs, etc. McDonnell Douglas integrates their ethics programs into their strategic planning process. Ethics management programs are also useful in managing diversity. Diversity is much more than the color of people's skin—it's acknowledging different values and perspectives. Diversity programs require recognizing and applying diverse values and perspectives—these activities are the basis of a sound ethics management program.

Ethics programs promote a strong public image. Attention to ethics is also strong public relations—admittedly, managing ethics should not be done primarily for reasons of public relations. But, frankly, the fact that an organization regularly gives attention to its ethics can portray a strong positive to the public. People see those organizations as valuing people more than profit, as striving to operate with the utmost of integrity and honor. Aligning behavior with values is critical to effective marketing and public relations programs. Consider how Johnson and Johnson handled the Tylenol crisis versus how Exxon handled the oil spill in Alaska. Bob Dunn, President and CEO of San Francisco-based Business for Social Responsibility, puts it best: "Ethical values, consistently applied, are the cornerstones in building a commercially successful and socially responsible business."

Consider the following guidelines when developing codes of ethics:

1. ***Review any values need to adhere to relevant laws and regulations;*** this ensures your organization is not (or is not near) breaking any of them. (If you are breaking any of them, you may be far better off to report this violation than to try hide the problem. Often, a reported violation generates more leniency than outside detection of an unreported violation, particularly per the new Federal Sentencing Guidelines.) Increase priority on values that will help your organization operate to avoid breaking these laws and to follow necessary regulations.

2. ***Review which values produce the top three or four traits of a highly ethical and successful product or service in your area,*** e.g., for accountants: objectivity, confidentiality, accuracy, etc. Identify which values produce behaviors that exhibit these traits.

3. *Identify values needed to address current issues in your workplace.* Appoint one or two key people to interview key staff to collect descriptions of major issues in the workplace. Collect descriptions of behaviors that produce the issues. Consider which of these issues is ethical in nature, e.g.., issues in regard to respect, fairness and honesty. Identify the behaviors needed to resolve these issues. Identify which values would generate those preferred behaviors. There may be values included here that some people would not deem as moral or ethical values, e.g., team-building and promptness, but for managers, these practical values may add more relevance and utility to a code of ethics.

4. *Identify any values needed, based on findings during strategic planning.* Review information from your SWOT analysis (identifying the organization's strengths, weaknesses, opportunities and threats). What behaviors are needed to build on strengths, shore up weaknesses, take advantage of opportunities and guard against threats?

5. *Consider any top ethical values that might be prized by stakeholders.* For example, consider expectations of employees, clients/customers, suppliers, funders, members of the local community, etc.

6. *Collect from the above steps, the top five to ten ethical values which are high priorities in your organization (see item #7 below for examples).*

7. *Examples of ethical values might include* (the following list is the "Six Pillars of Character" developed by The Josephson Institute of Ethics, 310-306-1868):
   a) *Trustworthiness:* honesty, integrity, promise-keeping, loyalty
   b) *Respect:* autonomy, privacy, dignity, courtesy, tolerance, acceptance
   c) *Responsibility:* accountability, pursuit of excellence
   d) *Caring:* compassion, consideration, giving, sharing, kindness, loving

e) *Justice and fairness:* procedural fairness, impartiality, consistency, equity, equality, due process

f) *Civic virtue and citizenship:* law abiding, community service, protection of environment

8. **Compose your code of ethics; attempt to associate with each value, two example behaviors which reflect each value.** Critics of codes of ethics assert that they seem vacuous because many only list ethical values and do not clarify these values by associating examples of behaviors.

9. **Include wording that indicates all employees are expected to conform to the values stated in the code of ethics.** Add wording that indicates where employees can go if they have any questions.

10. **Obtain review from key members of the organization.** Get input from as many members as possible.

11. **Announce and distribute the new code of ethics (unless you are waiting to announce it along with any new codes of conduct and associated policies and procedures).** Ensure each employee has a copy and post codes throughout the facility.

12. **Update the code at least once a year.** As stated several times in this document, the most important aspect of codes is developing them, not the code itself. Continued dialogue and reflection around ethical values produces ethical sensitivity and consensus. Therefore, revisit your codes at least once a year—preferably two or three times a year

CHAPTER 12 ANSWERS

1. *Size:* this refers to an organization's capacity, number of personnel, outputs, and resources.

Technology / Task: it appears that certain activities correspond with certain structures. For example, companies that make one-of-a-kind custom products, or small quantities (unit production/small batch) have few levels of hierarchy.

Environment: this refers to an organization's ability to adapt to its environment, its dependence on its customers and suppliers, and the process of natural selection of those companies that are well suited to their environment.

2. *Organizational Structure* (purpose, planning, profits, people, physical plant)
Product or Service Structure (production, processes)
Marketing Structure (presence, presentation)

3. The key benefit of global organizations is the ability to exploit regional differences in needs (customers) and production capabilities (worker expertise, costs, government aid, etc.)

4. *Globalization:* affects business in the movement from direct exports to having sales offices in different countries to having manufacturing to all functions spread across the globe, : increases international sales, manufacturing, research and development, and management, : due to a search for unsaturated markets, reduced cost and improved quality of international transportation and communication

Diversity: affects the workplace as a source of both innovation and conflict / communication problems, : presents a challenge to cope with different styles of interaction, dress, presentation, and physical appearance, : due to changing demographics and the globalization of the labor market.

Flat: affects business structure by establishing fewer levels of management,: workers are empowered to make decisions,: due to need for speed in making decisions, changes in information technology.

CHAPTER 13 ANSWERS

1. The five qualities of essence are:
   1. Intuition
   2. Will
   3. Joy
   4. Strength
   5. Compassion

2. The five traits that investors look for in an entrepreneur are
   1. Leadership
   2. Vision
   3. Integrity
   4. Openness
   5. Dedication

3. The 10 the *ten steps to an entrepreneurial organization* are:
   1. Give users of internal services a choice of more than one internal vendor.
   2. Give employees the security of something akin to ownership rights in the internal intraprises they create, as well as the larger corporation.
   3. Demand and engender truth and honesty, marketplace feedback and marketplace discipline, to support widespread decision-making.

4. Give intrapreneurial teams responsibility for their own bottom line even if they are subsidized—as a profit center rather than a cost center.

5. Allow many options and diversity in personnel, in jobs, in innovation efforts, alliances, exchanges.

6. Provide extensive training and education, and safety nets, so employees can develop and take risks as their organization develops.

7. Create an internal "bank account" for every internal enterprise.

8. Streamline systems for registering internal enterprises so they have standing in the corporation.

9. Establish a system for registering agreements and contracts between internal enterprises, so that people can give their word and trust the system.

10. Establish a justice system for adjudicating disputes between internal enterprises and between employees and enterprises.

CHAPTER 14 ANSWERS

1. Admission to a Governor's school is dependent on the qualifications of the student, who must be considered "gifted" and be nominated and approved by a state committee. Charter schools are open to anyone that operate free from many of the regulations of other public schools in return for a limited-time "charter" or contract that details student achievement. Both non-profit, public schools must strategically manage their funds. They must compete for some of the same available funds.

2. IRM stands for Information Resources Management, which is a branch of the Department of Health and Human Services. Four "drivers" of its strategic plan are: 1.) Health Care Reform 2.)

National Performance Review 3.) New Legislation 4.) Deficit Reduction

3. The Congress and the Executive Branch have provided the following three management tools to government agencies to aid their administrations in the achievement of their goals and objectives: 1.) The Government Performance and Results Act (GPRA)—is the principal tool that compels federal programs to focus on results 2.) Chief Financial Officer Act (CFOA)—assures financial accountability 3.) The Federal Acquisition Streamlining Act (FASA)—broke new ground in acquisition methodology and embodies key principals of acquisition reform.

CHAPTER 15 ANSWERS

1. The person would need an understanding of the cultural issues that are relevant to the knowledge creation processes; specifically the person should be able to facilitate a 'clan control' or 'self- control' based culture [with the help of the top management] that can facilitate dialog. The person would need to have a good grasp of the multiple perspectives on core issues and should be willing to relate to diverse perspectives [from various individuals] that are material to the knowledge creation process. Open-mindedness is essential along with the willingness and/or ability to act as a liaison between the top management's strategic needs and the staff level operational concerns.

2. In the United States, the Clinton administration took measures to amplify the Net's technical capabilities and availability manifold via the National Research and Education Network. France, with the world's largest national information utility, Minitel, and Japan, with

its stake in future telecommunications industries, have their own visions of the future. Albert Gore's 1991 bill, the High Performance Computing Act, signed into law by President Bush, outlined Gore's vision for "highways of the mind" to be stimulated by federal research-and-development expenditures as a national intellectual resource and carried to the citizens by private enterprise. The Clinton-Gore administration has used the example of the ARPA (Advanced Research Projects Agency) venture of the 1960s and 1970s that produced the Net and the foundations of personal computing as an example of the way they see government and the private sector interacting in regard to future communications technologies.

3. **a. Knowledge-based strategies begin with strategy, not knowledge.** The new form of intellectual capital is meaningless without the old-fashioned objectives of serving customers and beating competitors. If a company does not have its fundamentals in place, all the corporate learning, information technology, or knowledge databases are mere costly diversions. The old truth is still the best truth: a company has to know the kind of value it intends to provide and to whom. Only then can it link its knowledge resources in ways that make a difference: serving customers around the world in a coordinated, consistent manner; responding quickly and effectively to changing competitive conditions; and offering its products or services to customers more quickly, cheaply, efficiently, and innovatively. **b. Knowledge-based strategies aren't strategies unless you can link them to traditional measures of performance.** If knowledge can't be connected to measurable improvements in performance —including improvements on the bottom line—then the knowledge revolution will be short-lived, and deservedly so. Successes can be tracked

to the superior use of knowledge. The point of a knowledge-based strategy is not to save the world; it's to make money.

c. Executing a knowledge-based strategy is not about managing knowledge; it's about nurturing people with knowledge. Knowledge is also about soft hearts. And here's a key paradox. "Knowledge for knowledge's sake" lacks performance discipline; but efforts to engineer knowledge in some coldly bloodless way subvert the human dimensions of learning. The trick is to balance the "hard" with the "soft"—tapping the knowledge locked in people's experience. There is a corollary to the importance of tacit knowledge: people will not willingly share it with coworkers if their workplace culture does not support learning, cooperation, and openness.

d. Organizations leverage knowledge through networks of people who collaborate not through networks of technology that interconnect. Interconnectivity begins with people who want to connect. When it works the combination of people and technology produces networks of people who transform themselves into "worknets"— suborganizations or informal groups whose collective knowledge accomplishes a specific task. The key to this worknet transition is that its members have compelling reasons for finding others with knowledge to share who in turn have compelling reasons to share their knowledge when asked.

e. People networks leverage knowledge through organizational "pull" rather than centralized information "push." The engine that drives knowledge development and sharing is the worker's need for help in solving business problems; the power comes from the demand side rather than the supply side. The "pull-not-push" principle suggests that problems need to be framed and articulated specifically. For this reason, knowledge-based strategies should emphasize on-the-job learning rather than traditional training. "Just in time" learning, which takes place in the moment of actual need, not only creates the most value; it also makes the biggest impression on the learner and the organization. Ultimately, learning is up to each individual—it's not something that management can require. The essence of successful knowledge-based strategies is a company's capacity to raise the aspirations of each employee. These are the people whose contributions and ongoing development become the lifeblood of performance gains.

CHAPTER 16 ANSWERS

1. It is an excuse for management to lay off employees with the experience needed to produce quality to customers and enterprise growth for the future.

   It drives fear into the organization

   It destroys the social dimension of the sociotechnical system, which produces a product or service

2. Be customer-value driven. Develop a customer-driven business model and help align technology capabilities with business needs.

   Be an innovation leader. Be a catalyst for the application of new technology and partner in business process improvement.

   Create a standardized, open-systems environment and infrastructure that leverages common platforms.

3. Major business process change typically affects processes, technology, job roles, and culture in the workplace. Significant changes to even one of these areas require resources, money, and leadership. Changing them simultaneously is an extraordinary task. If top management does not provide strong and consistent support, most likely

one of these three elements (money, resources, or leadership) will not be present over the life of the project, severely crippling your chances for success. It may be true that consultants and reengineering managers give this topic a lot of attention. Mostly because current models of re-designing business processes use staff functions and consultants as change agents, and often the targeted organizations are not inviting the change. Without top management sponsorship, implementation efforts can be strongly resisted and ineffective. Top management support for large companies with corporate staff organizations has another dimension. If the top management in the "line" organization and "staff" organization do not partner and become equal stakeholders in the change, AND you only have staff management support, you most likely are ill-prepared for a successful reengineering project (line management in this context are the top managers of the operation ultimately accountable for business performance—P&L, customer service, etc.). Projects that result in major change in an organization rarely succeed without top management support in the line organization.

CHAPTER 17 ANSWERS

1. **Class I**—any combination of live and dead cells quickly approaches a steady equilibrium state. All cells are dead, therefore, life is extinguished

   Class II—the cells develop into static groupings (or patterns) of live cells. They may be groups of cells that oscillate between fixed states

   Class III—are chaotic. The cells alternate between 'on' and 'off' positions. There is no predictable patterns or stability.

Class IV—are coherent structures that propagate, grow, split apart, and are recombined in a complex manner. They are capable of producing extended transients and their behavior is stable and predictable with some degree of uncertainty

2. There were dramatic social changes. The urban renaissance, which began as welfare reform, became a more sweeping transformation. More and more cities aimed at reducing crime, reviving its inner core, creating jobs, and reducing poverty, drug abuse, and other social problems. There were radical efforts to improve public education, create parks, and other environmental amenities. There was a religious revival and expansion of social ministry of virtually every denomination to aid the effort. The Church-related groups provided the cities with public funds to deliver social services, support stressed families, and motivate job seekers and recovering alcoholics. Poverty declined and almost every social indicator showed improvement. Cities became attractive places to live and suburban areas' growth slowed. Global population peaked in 2040 and gradually declined afterwards.

3. A few rules guide the interaction between the components of a system. They include:
   1. Managers (in a business context) should attend to relationships at all levels within the organization.
   2. Small changes have large effects.
   3. Interesting and unpredictable properties can be expected to emerge from a system.

The result of these is it is difficult to implement a strategic plan long term. The complexity theory demonstrates that underlying principles found in nature apply to human organizations. To apply the complexity theory to strategic planning one must realize that strategic planning must be short term. One must also recognize the business environment as a complex system that is unpredictable and the failure of long term strategic planning is not failure of management, but an expected outcome of the business environment. Managers are challenged to feel comfortable by setting the direction for the future and to be ready to adapt and evolve as the environment changes.

CHAPTER 18 ANSWERS

1. a.) databases
   b.) pplications
   c.) interfaces
   d.) tools
   e.) BPR

2. a.) The first is to see the company's eBusiness platform as an extension of the existing brand without making significant changes to the underlying business.

   b.) The second option takes the first approach, but introduces structural changes to the underlying business.

   c.) The third approach is to launch the eBusiness platform as an entirely new entity, incorporating a different business model from the core business, as well as a different brand.

3. A great CRM strategy requires the following steps:
   a.) Realigns and reinvents business processes
      • Requires policy decisions that effect the online organization
      • Opens the enterprise for customer self-sale and self-service

b.) Is based upon the full range of technology
- Enables new business strategies
- Streamlines processes and speeds communication
- Adapts quickly to support business changes

c.) Provides a complete view of each customer

d.) Uses technology to make the most of each customer contact
- Each contact becomes an opportunity to sell
- Customers can use seller's processes instead of building their own

e.) Puts current applications to strategic use
- Data warehouse stores used to strategic advantages
- Back-office system integrated for customer support

f.) Drives ROI for both users and customers

CHAPTER 19 ANSWERS

1. a.) Serve as a framework for decisions or for securing support/approval.

   b.) Explain the business to others in order to inform, motivate, & involve.

   c.) Assist benchmarking and performance monitoring.

   d.) Stimulate change and become a building block for the next plan.

2. a.) quantitative

   b.) qualitative

   c.) exponential smoothing

   d.) regression analysis

   e.) sensitivity analysis

   f.) financial models

3. Financial ratio analysis is important because it helps to examine the current performance of your company in comparison to past periods of time, from the prior quarter to years ago. It also helps to point out potential problems which can be avoided. Also, the ratios help to compare the performance of your company against that of your competitors or other members of your industry.

CHAPTER 20 ANSWERS

1. a. identity
   b. vision
   c. organizational action
   d. configuration

2. a. a game plan
   b. a threat
   c. a pattern of behavior
   d. a position in the marketplace
   e. a perspective shared by members of the organization

3. The three factors are well-developed core competencies that serve as launch points for new products and services, an attitude that supports continuous improvement in the business's value-added chain, and the ability to fundamentally renew or revitalize. There are three assumptions which can be made from the factors listed above. The first is that an organization's ability to survive and grow is based on

advantages that stem from core competencies that represent collective learning. The second is that the value chain of any organization is a domain of integrated learning. The last assumption is that the learning process has three identifiable stages: knowledge acquisition, knowledge sharing, and knowledge utilization.

www.ingramcontent.com/pod-product-compliance
Lightning Source LLC
Chambersburg PA
CBHW030746180526
45163CB00003B/931